Successful
Public
Meetings

Elaine Cogan

Successful
Public
Meetings

A Practical Guide
for Managers
in Government

Jossey-Bass Publishers · San Francisco

For sales outside the United States contact Maxwell/Macmillan International Publishing Group, 866 Third Avenue, New York, New York 10022

Printed on acid-free paper and manufactured in the United States of America

Library of Congress Cataloging-in-Publication Data

Cogan, Elaine, date.
    Successful public meetings : a practical guide for managers in government / Elaine Cogan. — 1st ed.
        p.   cm. — (The Jossey-Bass public administration series)
    Includes bibliographical references and index.
    ISBN 1-55542-403-1
    1. Public meetings.   I. Title.   II. Series.
JF1525.P8C55   1992
350.81'9—dc20   91-30035
                                                                                    CIP

FIRST EDITION
HB Printing   10 9 8 7 6 5 4 3 2 1   *Code 9208*

The Jossey-Bass
Public Administration Series

To my husband, Arnold, with love

*If everyone conducted meetings as well as you do,
there would be no need for this book.*

Contents

Preface

This book began as a gleam in the eye of my editor, who called me one day to say, "I've heard of your workshops on how to hold effective meetings. There doesn't seem to be anything definitive published on that subject. How would you like to write a book?"

His query started me thinking about unsuccessful public meetings, which at best are merely boring and at worst are political or bureaucratic disasters. Most of us have been in meetings when citizens became hostile after being treated in a demeaning or condescending manner by political leaders, technical experts, or representatives of public agencies. We have seen panel discussions that dragged on way beyond their time limit because the speakers ignored the schedule and moderators abdicated their responsibility to keep things on track. We have suffered through audiovisual presentations that were too long or too complicated.

We probably have also witnessed, or even participated in, some outstanding public meetings — meetings at which everything seemed to work out. A successful meeting is the reward for studious attention to many factors; it is not the result of luck or happenstance.

As a writer and consultant in communications, I have been working for some time with executives and managers of public agencies to facilitate public meetings that produce the desired results, both for my clients and for the public. I have also been working with executives and managers to design and conduct training workshops in this field.

There is considerable literature about components of successful meetings, such as techniques for facilitating discussion or for reaching agreement in difficult or contentious situations. Each method has its adherents and some record of success, but each is just as likely to fail in the wrong context or environment. A ready reference is needed to address the totality of factors — the host of minor and major details that stand between success and failure.

When read from beginning to end, this book gives the manager or executive a full accounting of everything needed to hold a satisfactory public meeting. Those who do not want to peruse the entire book but want specific information on matters such as how to work with the media or facilitate a discussion can turn to a particular section.

Organization of the Book

Chapter One rightly concerns leadership, the most important factor in ensuring the success of any public meeting. Agency directors or managers can motivate staff people to do a superior job only if they themselves understand the importance of attending to all the details. They must then transmit this understanding to their staffs in words and deeds, delegate the responsibility appropriately, and allocate all the necessary resources.

Leadership is also a prime ingredient of success at the meeting itself, as descriptions of the distinct roles and qualifications of the chairperson, facilitator, and discussion leader attest. The planners of the public meeting should be candid when assigning various leadership roles and consider the ability of each of the participants. If, for example, the mayor must be the convener because of political realities or tradition but lacks the skills to do a good job as facilitator, the role should be circumscribed sufficiently so that the smooth flow of the meeting is maintained. Title should not automatically confer status.

Chapter Two, on types of public meetings, makes the point that no single meeting can serve all purposes; thus it is important that organizers decide, at the outset of planning, on the meeting's primary goal. They need to define the purpose carefully, so that all that follows — the material sent to the public, the structure and format of the presentations and discussion, and the follow-up — are appropriate to the meeting's aims. Certainty and consistency are major factors in gaining and keeping public trust and acceptance.

Chapters Three and Four explain details that are essential to the success of any public meeting yet too many meeting planners ignore: effective ways first to notify the public and then to create a compatible environment once people are there. The importance of promising only as much as one can deliver and providing an atmosphere conducive to reaching the articulated goals cannot be overly stressed. Readers will have greater empathy for international negotiators who haggle over the shape of the conference table when they realize the effect of such details on the successful outcome of their meetings.

Dedicating adequate time for planning the meeting is a continual message of *Successful Public Meetings* and this certainly includes the actual presentations of staff and others. Though rank in the organization is frequently a factor in choosing who speaks when, it should not be the only consideration. Knowledge of the subject is important, of course, but so is the ability to present information clearly and succinctly to laypeople. Because that ability is rarely innate, numerous useful techniques are explained in Chapter Five.

With the advent of computers that can produce complex graphic displays, too many novices believe that they can be instant artists. Instead, most amateurs turn out mediocre charts, graphs, and other works — *more* audiovisuals but not *better*. Audiovisual aids of any type must be part of the overall planning for the meeting so that appropriate techniques are chosen, and they must be executed carefully so that they advance the audience's understanding of the subject. For easy reference, much of Chapter Six is presented in chart form. The chart summarizes advantages, disadvantages, and usage guidelines for each audiovisual technique.

Apathetics, hair-splitters, know-it-alls, sneak-outers — these and many other types of people likely to be encountered at a public meeting are described in detail in Chapter Seven. Chairpeople and facilitators must always treat each participant with respect, but they must also be firm in advancing the aims of the meeting and guarding the rights of the majority.

The media are another audience with whom meeting planners must deal. Chapter Eight shows how understanding the differing objectives and requirements of the press, radio, and television can help meeting planners obtain more fair and adequate coverage. What to do when the media err and how and to whom to address complaints are also discussed.

The book concludes with a definitive checklist for meeting planners, covering everything that needs to be done before, during, and after the public meeting. There are no shortcuts to success — only the experience garnered by using techniques that work.

Throughout the book I've used examples to illustrate specific ideas or concepts. As bizarre as some of the stories may seem, they are all real; each one happened sometime — most often to hapless public officials who should have known better.

At this crucial time in the life of our democratic society, when the public is becoming more sophisticated and vocal about playing an active role in public policy, administrators and their staffs, and the political processes they serve, must be informed about how to hold effective public meetings and be willing to allocate the personnel and financial resources to getting the job done right.

Portland, Oregon   Elaine Cogan
November 1991

The Author

Elaine Cogan is a partner in the Portland, Oregon, planning and communications consulting firm of Cogan Sharpe Cogan. She has designed and facilitated hundreds of public meetings: from the 1960s when she calmed down gun-waving activists who threatened a few dozen participants at neighborhood meetings to the late 1980s when she involved thousands of citizens in twenty-six communities to help solve the problems of financing public elementary and secondary education. In 1991, the citizen involvement program she designed as part of the city of Portland's Future Focus strategic planning process received special recognition by the U.S. Conference of Mayors when the conference gave the city an "Outstanding Achievement" award. She believes in and practices a philosophy that minimizes confrontation, encourages all participants to air their views, and produces a consensus that everyone can support.

As a consultant to a fast-growing suburb of Portland, Cogan developed and facilitated an Envision Gresham project to guide the community's future growth and development. A unique component of the process involved the youth of the city as "Young Visionaries." The project has received national recognition. She also has been retained by Governor Barbara Roberts of Oregon to design a far-reaching conversation project, a process to involve the governor and thousands of citizens in discussing and reaching consensus on vital public policy matters.

Cogan is the coauthor (with B. Padrow, 1984) of *You Can Talk to (Almost) Anyone About (Almost) Anything: A Speaking Guide for Business and Professional People* and is an advisor and consultant to public agencies throughout the United States. She understands the media well, having been an editorial columnist for the *Oregon Journal* and *Oregonian* newspapers and a producer/moderator of a radio talk show. In addition to her consultant work, she is a TV and radio commentator on political issues.

A native of Brooklyn, New York, and a graduate of Oregon State University, Cogan is a member of the national honorary societies Phi Kappa Phi and Omicron Nu.

Successful
Public
Meetings

Introduction

When You Have
to Face the Public

Most executives or managers of public agencies cringe at the very idea of holding or participating in a public meeting — and for good reason! Public meetings are unpredictable. They are messy. They often become arenas where people confront each other on issues that they would rather avoid. They can be time-consuming to organize and boring and tedious to attend, taking precious time away from matters that managers would rather address — such as getting on with the project or process.

Given the generally unsatisfactory nature of most public meetings, it is no wonder that executives and their staff people face the prospect with the same dread they feel when they go to the dentist: they may have to do it, but they do not have to like it. But while the dentist is prepared for unwilling clients and can deal with their shortcomings, the citizenry is not and will not. People become cranky or even downright obstreperous if public agencies subject them to meetings that do not meet their expectations.

Despite our resistance or aversion, there are many compelling reasons to hold a public meeting (defined here as any

1

gathering of elected and/or appointed officials attended or participated in by the public). The most prevalent reason is administrative or legal: you may have to. In many cases, political
jurisdictions must sponsor public meetings or hearings as part
of the process of informing and obtaining the approval of their
constituencies. The open public forum is an accepted part of
doing the public's business. For example, the federal government requires hearings to obtain public comment before funds
are allocated for, among other things, highway projects, forest
practices, and enforcement of food and drug policies; the U.S.
Forest Service and other agencies have involved processes for
environmental impact studies for proposed land-use changes and
other matters. Most local and state governments have similar
procedures. Yet even these pro forma public hearings can be
made innovative and interesting, as we will see in further chapters.

Another reason to hold a public meeting is strategic or
political. Even when you are not required to invite the public
into the deliberations, it may be a very good idea if you do.
Enlisting the public as a partner or owner of the process or
product can help you defuse potential opposition, acquire al-
lies in unlikely places, and unite a community and its leaders
around a common purpose. It also builds trust. The process of
holding an effective public meeting can itself be a product. When
people carry away good feelings and positive attitudes, they have
confidence in the public agency that can be a cornerstone for
other projects and programs.

Bad meetings do happen to good people, but the over-
riding premise of this book is that successful meetings happen
not only if the stars are arrayed in the right place in the heavens;
most often, they are the result of hard work and a recognition
by those in charge of the delicate balance between success and
failure. Even if their overworked staff members balk at first,
managers must be firm in dedicating the time and resources to
carrying out even the small, but important, details. Just one
major success is enough to make believers of even the most reluctant individuals.

Well, then, what are measurements of success? How can
we tell when we have had a constructive and effective public

meeting? The most immediate and accurate indicator is our own feelings when it is over. We may be tired, even exhausted; we may wish that we had answered a particular question differently or chosen a more suitable chart or graph. But if we know that the meeting has been productive and interesting and that the audience has had a good time, we can feel satisfied.

None of this just happens, however; it is the result of an ongoing three-part process: premeeting planning, careful execution, and debriefing.

Planning is essential to the success of every public meeting. If you treat the meeting as an add-on to an already over-burdened schedule, gather up slides at the last minute and stuff them into a slide tray, ask any staff person who happens to be free to make a presentation, take whatever location is available without checking it out, get to the room with no idea whether you will face an audience of 20 or 200 — in other words, if you have a cavalier attitude toward the public meeting — you court disaster. We laugh when we read of diplomats who spend weeks arguing over room size and the configuration of tables and chairs before they settle down to discuss weighty international issues, but we would sympathize more if we realized how crucial these factors are to our own success.

In planning your public meeting, the first question to ask yourself is: why are we having it? Managers and their top assistants, as well as any staff members who are actively involved with gathering data or meeting with citizens on the issue, need to get together for an honest assessment. The purpose of the public meeting may be informational, advisory, decision-making, or some combination thereof. The format and structure should be developed only after you have ascertained the reason for the meeting. Ask yourself: what public purpose will be served? If some decision has already been made behind closed doors and you hope that the public will benignly give its blessing, for example, it may be better not to hold the meeting at all. Instead, you could talk with small groups of influential people to convince them to support your efforts.

After you have decided that there are sufficient reasons to hold the meeting, choose the team that will be responsible for the event and divide up responsibilities. Team leaders should not necessarily be the technical people who have the best data or information on the subject under discussion. In fact, technicians often do not possess the appropriate meeting-organizational skills. Your team should consist of at least the following:

- Agency director to lead the way in setting overall goals and objectives and to solve policy issues.
- Meeting manager skilled in group dynamics and able to deal with all the important factors that make a meeting a success.
- Unflappable assistant in charge of logistics and such details as finding a suitable location, notification, name tags, food, and handouts.
- Media liaison who understands the requirements of the press, radio, and television.
- Chair, moderators, facilitators, technical presenters, and others as the format requires.
- One or more people who understand the project or the process and can bring a needed political or historical perspective.
- Experts in presentation and audiovisual techniques.

The team should have its initial meeting six weeks before the event and draw up a detailed schedule of activities, including deadlines and responsibilities.

There are often minimum legal requirements that underlie notification procedures — for example, having to apprise all property owners within a certain distance of a local proposed development — but the wise meeting planner reaches out further. Even if you use an extensive and up-to-date list, if your notice is reader-unfriendly, you may motivate few people to attend your meeting. Most official notices are so packed with legalese and jargon that citizens take one glance and throw them away in disgust, only to find out later that a public matter has been approved against their wishes. The public official may retort smugly, "It's too late. Where were you? We sent you a notice," but this may not be enough to mollify angry citizens; they may mount recall campaigns, take legal action, or find other recourse for their feelings of betrayal. Public agencies certainly must follow the statutory requirements for public notice, but in many cases they should take further steps to reach people who may be concerned.

To adapt an architectural expression, the format of a meeting should always follow its function. If meetings organized by your office have always been done a certain way, but the reason is lost in antiquity, have the courage to analyze their effectiveness and be willing to organize them another way more suited to today's needs.

Before you choose your format, identify the needs of your audience. Wise meeting planners avoid the pitfall of having only one approach or process that they trot out for all occasions. Recognize, too, that few staff people or public officials are appropriate presenters for all occasions. Some relate very well to neighborhood shirtsleeve meetings but freeze with fright if they have to make formal presentations to large groups. Others enjoy the on-stage aspects of the latter and hate to meet people eye to eye. Only after a careful analysis of your audience should you choose the appropriate program, process, and participants.

The purpose of this book is to inspire managers and leaders to cut loose from the déjà vu school of meeting planning, even if it has worked (or at least kept you and your organization out of serious trouble) the last 255 times. While the primary reason to consider other ways of doing things is to gain more certain public participation and acceptance, an important by-product is to motivate and inspire your own staff. Conscientious executives will appreciate the team-building aspects of this approach to meeting management. As staff people work together intensively, they develop a communal spirit and a respect for each other that can carry into other aspects of work.

Good meeting planning only gets you there, however. Lack of attention to effective presentation, an uncertain or dogmatic chair, facilitators who ignore carefully developed schedules and agendas, inept audiovisuals, and general sloppiness will counteract the most meticulous premeeting efforts.

Technical experts are good in their place: to present data or complicated information. But they must be kept to strict time

limits and not be allowed to drone on and on without proper
visual aids and the assistance of people who can speak a language that the audience understands. An effective public meeting agenda has room for the experts but also assigns clear roles
to the chair, facilitators, presenters, recorders, and the audience.

As is discussed in later chapters, there are many ways to
involve the public and give people a sense of ownership in the
process and the result. It is important that you create and maintain an environment in which the public feels safe and comfortable when making comments—even comments with which
others may disagree.

In addition to willingly committing time and staff resources to planning and developing public meetings, managers
and executives can make another important contribution to success by exuding a sense of excitement and anticipation. As you
develop meeting-organizational skills, you will begin to enjoy
these previously dreaded events and be able to communicate
your enjoyment to your staff and the audience.

Premeeting planning and meeting execution are two of
the three parts of the process. The third is the postmeeting
debriefing. If you are not too exhausted after the meeting is over,
go out for coffee, dessert, or a pizza with all the staff participants and perhaps even interested elected officials or friendly
citizens, or schedule a half-hour or so the next day for recap.
While the details are still fresh in everyone's mind, be candid
with each other. What worked? What did not? If you were in
a large room, could everyone see the audiovisuals? Are there
ways that you could have defused those hostile questions with
more ease? Did the right people make the presentations, or did
Frank's stage fright show too much? (Maybe he is better behind the scenes and would be relieved to have someone else make
the presentation next time.) Did you overhear any audience comments that were helpful? Learn from your mistakes as well as
your successes and you will do even better next time.

For more specific guidelines, read on!

1

Leadership: The Key to Successful Public Meetings

The single most important ingredient in assuring the success of a public meeting is clear and decisive leadership. Every factor described further in this book—correct format, receiver-friendly notice, appropriate environment, clear presentations, positive media relationships, and all the rest—are additional essential elements in helping you have a successful public meeting. But citizens endure all manner of inconvenience and forgive those inevitable glitches if they believe in their leaders. Conversely, the most ideal setting and circumstances cannot make up for inadequate leadership. The audience gives meeting sponsors and presenters a precious possession: its time. A good leader appreciates that and uses it wisely. Managers or executives can and should delegate many aspects of organizing and running meetings, but they need to realize that they alone can set the scene for success.

Effective leaders understand the dynamic tension between content and context, between what is communicated and how it is communicated. It is easier to find the experts to provide the date and information you need than to design the process

7

that will enable people to work together in a positive environment to discuss difficult issues or solve problems. As is discussed in Chapter Two, on types of public meetings, there are many ways to deal with the same issue. Leaders need to work with staff members to find the right process for this particular time, place, audience, and subject.

At the public meetings that are the subject of this book, there are two common leadership roles: the chairperson and the facilitator. The highest-ranking individual at the meeting, the chair, is responsible for representing the sponsoring agency or group and presiding over the agenda—particularly the beginning and ending. The chair greets and introduces people and sets the general tone. The facilitator then assumes the task of making it all happen as planned and directing the flow of information and discussion. Recorders, discussion leaders, resource people, and others take their cues from the facilitator, though they may be introduced by the chair. While in some cases one individual can take both roles, it is usually advisable to divide up the duties.

Attributes of Leadership

Both the chairperson and the facilitator must be conversant with the subjects under discussion. While they leave the details to others, they should know enough about the issues to detect when the discussion is getting off the track and to recognize when disrupters promulgate false or misleading information.

Leaders must also show fairness and be able to leave any strong personal opinions behind as they mount the podium. They may have to be firm in keeping to the agenda and schedule, but always within a context that treats all citizens equitably and with goodwill.

In a democracy, true leadership comes by minimizing, not accentuating, the trappings of power. The presidential seal travels wherever the president of the United States goes and is placed on the podium before he speaks; but his ability to lead comes from what he says, not who he is. Some dignitaries flaunt flags, banners, assistants, and sycophants as evidence of their importance. Others create a distance between themselves and the public by sitting on a raised stage or dais yards away. These devices will backfire and alienate citizens from their leaders if there is no substance to back them up. If the public does not feel that it is being treated with respect, it will find a way to fight back, whether by disrupting the proceedings, taking to the streets before or after, voting nay on specific issues at the ballot box, turning the rascals out of office, or resorting to the courts.

Effective leaders know how to maintain the proper balance between formality and informality. Those who rule exclusively by the book are most likely insecure. Though their arrogant manners would lead us to believe that they are self-confident, the opposite is true; they hide behind an unreasonably strict structure and discourage citizen participation and interaction because they are afraid that the meeting will get out of their control. They use time as a weapon: having allowed their chosen experts to monopolize the agenda, they then claim that there is not enough time to give the public a chance to speak. They run the meeting solely in the interest of their agency or themselves.

At the other extreme, casual, laid-back, anything-goes leaders are anarchists at heart. They may make the audience feel good at the time, but the public often feels betrayed after the euphoria wears off and people realize that nothing was accomplished.

Leaders who have energy and enthusiasm, who are upbeat and positive, are forgiven many other faults. People want to follow leaders whose sense of excitement is revealed by their words and deeds. On the other hand, leaders with low energy convey apathy and disinterest. These attributes are also contagious, but in a negative way.

Effective leaders use praise unsparingly. They do not hesitate to compliment individuals without passing judgment on the content of their remarks: "Jesse, we certainly appreciate your reminding us of the history of our neighborhood; it puts an interesting perspective on the issues we're talking about tonight." It is not necessary for the leader to indicate whether she likes or dislikes Jesse's "perspective." It is more important that her

words praise the old-timer for being willing to make a contribution to the discussion.

The Chairperson

Executives, managers, directors, mayors, or other political
leaders are the most logical choice to chair public meetings. They
should participate in planning by helping to decide the broad
objectives and general process of the meeting and then take part
in the dress rehearsal, while delegating the details of the preplan-
ning to subordinates. Details of the meeting itself should also
be delegated. If the projector light burns out or the microphone
is having feedback problems, for example, others should have
been assigned to take care of them. The chair has enough to
do being the host, greeting people, and making everyone feel
comfortable. This host function is especially important if the
subject of the meeting is controversial or if some attendees are
expected to be contentious or antagonistic. The most effective
technique for disarming the opposition is to stand at the door
as people come in, smile at friend and foe alike, greet them by
name (if you know it), and extend an open hand. The most effective way to feed the opposition's paranoia and destructive ten-
dencies and ensure that antagonists will try to obstruct the
process is to turn away when you see them coming or be too
busy with housekeeping details to give them respect.

If at all possible, the chair should be introduced to the
media before the meeting. Someone else should be charged with
finding media representatives and bringing them over, but the
chair should be available for interviews and comments. On the
other hand, the chair should not delay starting the meeting on
time because of a lengthy media interview. Instead, he or she
should agree to be available at the first opportunity to continue
the interview — perhaps after opening the meeting or during the
break.

The chair sets the tone for a well-ordered meeting by beginning and ending on time. Any delay should be for a very
good reason. Sparse attendance is not one of them, as the expected number of people may never show up. Moreover, by

beginning within five minutes of the scheduled time, the chair respects those who followed the rules and shows latecomers that they miss something by being tardy. In the opening remarks, the chair can make everyone feel welcome and at ease by following this outline:

Never assume that everyone knows you. Introduce yourself: "Good evening, I'm glad to see so many familiar faces. I hope that by the end of the meeting we'll all get to know each other. I'm Jenny Goldman, your city planning director and chair of this evening's meeting." Then go on to say something personal that begins to build a bridge to your audience: "I've been in Plainview for five years, and it makes my job easier when citizens such as yourselves care to spend time talking about the important issues that are on tonight's agenda." Note the friendly neutrality of her remarks. She indicates her loyalty to the community and compliments the citizens for participating, without prejudging what they might want to say.

Next, review the purpose, agenda, and ground rules of the meeting. If you are taking testimony only from people who have registered beforehand, say so. Tell people if they can submit written remarks and how those remarks will be used. If there will be time for general discussion or small-group breakouts, tell participants when that will be. People want certainty and respect just as much as they want involvement. They will honor any reasonable agenda, if they are told beforehand what it is in a manner that assures them that everyone will be treated fairly.

It is important also to explain the logistics, particularly the location of the restrooms and microphones, and when and where any refreshments may be available. Let the audience know of any restrictions on parking that may cause offending cars to be towed.

Every community has political or other celebrities. If they are attending the meeting, make sure that your assistant has written down all their names, spelled correctly, so that you can introduce them. Be sure that all titles are correct and that you are able to pronounce the names without stumbling. Have some idea where they are sitting so that you can point generally in their direction. Do not invite them to speak unless it is a strategic necessity, and discourage all applause, even at the end— this is a serious public meeting, not a performance. If there are people you need to acknowledge who are not there, save them for last: "Having introduced our mayor and the chief of police, I now want to mention that the regional welfare supervisor had a last-minute change of schedule that kept him away. He told me to be sure to give you his warm greetings and said that he was anxious to read all your comments."

After these preliminaries, introduce the facilitator, who then takes over the meeting and introduces others, such as resource people or discussion leaders. Then you should retire unobtrusively from the front of the room instead of standing or sitting within view. It is important to be inconspicuous until the end of the meeting; do not disrupt the proceedings by holding court in a corner with a few cronies or favorite citizens. This is an opportune time to be interviewed by the media, but only if you find a corridor or another room away from the primary action. Some chairpeople, truly having no part to play in the proceedings, leave the premises and return near the end. This is acceptable if they leave quietly and come back in enough time to be briefed on anything unexpected that may have occurred in their absence. In a potentially volatile situation, however, it is smarter for chairpeople to remain nearby to be ready to make any necessary last-minute executive decisions. Moreover, by listening quietly, the chair can observe what the more active staff members may overlook. It is important, however, that the chair not seem to diminish or call into question the authority of the facilitator or others who have been given the responsibility of running the meeting.

The chair takes center stage again before the end of the meeting only when a problem such as a demonstration or disruption calls for a higher authority. How the chair makes an unscheduled appearance is a matter of preference and ability. Neutral, highly regarded chairpeople who have had no part in the heated proceedings may deal well with conflicts and field hostile questions diplomatically, while more partisan chairpeople may appear only to fan the flames. If they can maintain a neutral demeanor, chairpeople can speak for the policy of the agency with more certainty than either the facilitator or the resource people.

The chair's summary should include a short overview of what occurred at the meeting and what will happen next. Is this the only public discussion of the issue? Will there be others? Where and when? How will the agency use or respond to the citizens' comments received at this meeting? Will the outcome of this meeting become part of a report to be given to other decision makers? Are there opportunities for further written comments? Will minutes be sent to all participants, or can people pick up a recap somewhere? What are the next steps? If the chair feels too uninformed to make a meaningful summary, the facilitator can do it, but someone must summarize and tie up all the loose ends before the meeting is over.

It is as important to have a structure for closing as it is for opening. Always end when scheduled, even if there seems to be unfinished business. When you called the meeting, you made a pact with the audience for a particular time and format, and they have every right to expect you to keep your word. Time can be an ally if the meeting is being disrupted by angry or hostile people: "I know that there are still some issues we haven't addressed, but we promised to end at nine-thirty and it's nine–twenty-five. We have to wind up now, but I'll be glad to stay later to speak to you individually."

Before you make a graceful exit, thank everyone for coming and assure people how much you value their participation.

The Facilitator

The chair is the scene setter; the facilitator is the enabler. Discussion leaders, resource people, and all the others important to well-functioning meetings get their cues from the facilitator. The role of the facilitator is to stimulate, organize, and synthesize the thinking of the group so that it can reach consensus. Sometimes an agreement to disagree may be the best that can be attained, but the facilitator helps the group go as far as it can, without ridiculing, arguing, or ignoring anyone's point of view.

The most easy facilitation is with a group of twenty-five or fewer, when the facilitator can see people eye to eye and engage them individually as well as collectively. If the group numbers in the hundreds, successful facilitation is often primarily a case of fielding questions graciously from as many people as possible in the time allowed.

It is best to divide a large group into smaller units, if genuine discussion and analysis of alternatives is desired. Each group can then be led by a discussion leader, with the group facilitator responsible for the overall conduct of the meeting. With large groups or small, preparation, patience, and a positive attitude are the necessary attributes.

It is important to know the material well enough to understand when the discussion is going off on unproductive tangents. Don't be too focused, however: be accepting of different points of view and patient with slow thinkers or people who have difficulty expressing themselves.

Good facilitators and discussion leaders maintain a healthy balance between friendliness and firmness. Benevolence should not be construed as permission for someone who wants to dominate the meeting. The facilitator should use the agenda to keep the group from straying: "Yes, Mary, I can see that your idea would be a good one if we were talking about sewers, but tonight we're trying to decide how we should spend our park budget. What's your opinion about that?"

It is important to take the pulse of the group regularly so that you do not push people into polarization or force them to make premature decisions. Aim for consensus and general areas of agreement that allow everyone to come away with something rather than a vote in which there will be clear winners and losers. Give credence to differences, but do not let them bog down the process: "We seem to disagree on that point, but I noticed everyone nodding on the other issues. Let's see, then. We have consensus on items one, two, and four."

The leader aids the group process by continually paraphrasing and synthesizing: "If we combine Jim's idea of doubling the number of benches with Florence's about adding cookstoves, are we suggesting that we want a new picnic area?" Make sure participants nod or show their agreement before you move on. Remain alert to when the group has exhausted the subject and is willing to discuss another issue. Wrap it up when it is obvious that people have nothing more to say.

Facilitators must always resist the temptation to voice their own opinions and should never argue or allow others to engage in an argument: "Getting out various points of view is what this process is all about. Now that we've heard from Marie and Frank, let's go around the table and see what the rest of us have to say about this."

On the other hand, good facilitators are not afraid to say that they do not know. If you are asked a technical question that requires an answer before the discussion can proceed, try to find a resource person in the room. If no one knows, or if the answer really does not make a difference in the delibera-tions, indicate this tactfully: "I'm sorry no one seems to know the answer to that now, but let's assume that the budget will be the same as last year. What priorities would you all suggest?"

Use various techniques to stimulate or control discussion. If things bog down, try schoolteacher style: "When you hear the words *clean environment,* what comes to your mind?" Direct: "What do you think of when you hear the words *clean environment,* Jason?" Follow-up: "Peter, I see you're nodding. What's your opinion of what Jason said?" If you have an enthusiastic group in which everyone talks at once, introduce some order: "Let's see, we're going to have to slow down if everyone is to get a chance. I think Clarence had his hand up first, then Hortense, and then Elizabeth." Or, "Everyone obviously has something to say about this. Let's go around the table, starting with Robert."

While facilitators must never disavow the democratic process, they must be willing to make procedural decisions with-out entertaining a long discussion: "We have an hour to dis-cuss three topics, but the last one—funding—is more compli-cated, so I'm going to allot more time to it unless anyone objects."

Above all, the best facilitators keep cool, calm, and in command.

The Recorder

As noted in Chapter 2, recorders are essential only in problem-solving meetings. Whenever they are used, their role is to take notes, using a board or overhead projector, that are visible to all participants. Some facilitators prefer to be their own recorders, while others welcome an extra pair of eyes, ears, and hands. The role of the recorder is to show all participants that their opinions are being given credence and permanence by writing them down; to depersonalize the discussion for future use by not attributing anyone's name to the ideas and comments; to provide a sense of continuity and movement; to give newcomers the opportunity to catch up without having to interrupt the discussion; and to provide a visible record and point of reference for all.

If a verbatim transcript is required, hire trained court reporters. Otherwise, be selective when paraphrasing individual comments and the overall discussion so that they are not lost in a sea of details. The best recorders for public meetings are not stenographers trained to ignore content but astute recorders who can synopsize impartially. To assist recorders in their task, the meeting organizer should make sure that they understand the context and general language of the discussion and are attuned to the nuances of the subject and alert to the circuitous path the discussion may take.

Reporters must also be able to assimilate diverse ideas rapidly and accurately. They are the servants, not the masters, of the process and should not make a habit of holding up the discussion because they cannot keep up. Once in a while, it is acceptable to ask, "Let me see, before I write it down — I think I heard three separate points here," and then to paraphrase them. This enables the recorder and the group to catch up with each other. In general, however, recorders may very well run out of breath before the group runs out of ideas. That is a hazard that goes with the job.

Facilitators and recorders must maintain a good working relationship. This is more easily accomplished if they agree on the ground rules ahead of time. Will the facilitators synthesize the information for the recorders, or are the latter more or less on their own? How much information will be recorded, and when? Are the recorders to be seen and not heard, or may they interrupt (within reason, of course)?

It is important to be flexible as well. Recorders do not "own" their information and should not be possessive about it. The written record belongs to all the discussants, who have the right to change it until it accurately reflects their ideas.

A sense of humor can often defuse a tense or potentially volatile situation. This trait is important to all leaders, but particularly to recorders, who may be blamed unfairly when the message that they write carries bad news.

In addition to all these admirable traits, effective meeting leaders — chairpeople, facilitators, and recorders — have a sixth sense that keeps them and their meetings out of trouble. While that sense cannot be taught explicitly, it is nurtured when attention is paid to all the other attributes discussed in the chapters that follow.

2

Understanding
Different Types of
Public Meetings

Federal, state, and local boards; commissions, committees, task forces, forums, workshops; appointed, self-appointed, elected; ten attendees, twenty, two hundred — all public meetings are convened for one of three general purposes: informational, advisory, or problem solving. The first matter to consider in planning any meeting is its primary objective. The structure and organization of the meeting should be appropriate to carrying out this objective. If you have secondary objectives, they should be considered also.

Informational Meetings

Some public meetings are held primarily to convey information or data to decision-making bodies or to the public. Examples are legislative or administrative hearings, sessions of elected officials, and meetings of citizen groups such as neighborhood or civic organizations.

The communication between people at informational meetings is generally one-way — from the presenters to the audience.

18

Although the former are usually professional staff, they may be outside experts. Questions may be asked of the individuals who provide information, but an ongoing dialogue with the audience is discouraged. If the public is allowed to testify or present formal remarks, individuals are usually asked to sign up in advance, state their name, address, and affiliation, and speak within strict time limits. Verbatim transcripts may be taken, often to become part of a legally supportable written document. Informational meetings in community settings such as neighborhoods are less formal in structure than those before political decision makers in downtown civic buildings, but even they are characterized by a minimal amount of interaction among participants.

Though the environment and format of informational meetings are not receptive to surprises or creative ideas, some people find ways to break through.

In Oregon some time ago, Senator Maurine Neuberger took a skillful detour from the common, dry style that characterizes most testimony and won an important political victory. Faced with the competing interests of a predominantly male state legislature whose members had little experience in the kitchen, a female constituency clamoring for a change in the law to allow grocers to sell colored margarine, and an influential dairy lobby that did not want margarine to compete with butter, Senator Neuberger orchestrated an effective show-and-tell. On the polished mahogany table of the crowded legislative hearing room, she placed paraphernalia that disgruntled housewives all over the state faced: mixing bowls and spoons, white margarine, and little packets of yellow food coloring. Donning an apron over her dress-for-success suit, she fussed with the concoction, finally coloring the margarine the only way it was then allowed in the state — mixed in a bowl with a heavy spoon. She held up her messy results, having made her point effectively in front of her colleagues as well as the dozens of television, radio, and newspaper reporters she had alerted beforehand. The dairy lobby could not stem the tide of publicity and the law was changed to allow colored margarine to be sold in Oregon.

Individual Presentations

The most common form of presentation at an informational
meeting is one-way: one person at a time talks to a panel of
listeners. This "talking head" approach need not be, but often
is, dry. Part of the problem is that too many staff people who
have to present the same type of information at several meetings make the mistake of having a one-format-fits-all approach.
Each audience is different and requires a personalized presentation. This variation can be accomplished easily by reorganiz-
ing the same material to emphasize the concerns of each particular audience.

> *In the matter of a new zoning ordinance that permits mul-
> tiple-family dwellings in residential areas, for example, a
> city board of supervisors is most interested in how the pro-
> posal affects the budget for the planning department, while
> residents in a middle-class neighborhood are interested pri-
> marily in how it affects property values and traffic conges-
> tion. Wise presenters craft specific introductions that ac-
> knowledge the known concerns of each particular audience
> before presenting their other facts.*

As Figure 2.1 shows, in the typical hearing format, the
officials receiving the information are seated on a raised platform,
removed from the audience. Even if they are on the same level
as the spectators, there is a noticeable distance between them.

If you are speaking to such a body, give them your primary attention, no matter how many people are passively watching the proceedings behind you. Make sure that any visual aids,
such as charts or slides, are also directed toward the decision
makers or sponsors of the meeting. If possible, arrange the screen
or charts at an angle so that they can be seen by both the public
officials and the general public; but if you have to make a choice,
the officials who are your primary audience come first. Use handouts to emphasize particular points or to provide additional information that can be read later. Have a sufficient quantity for
all the expected attendees.

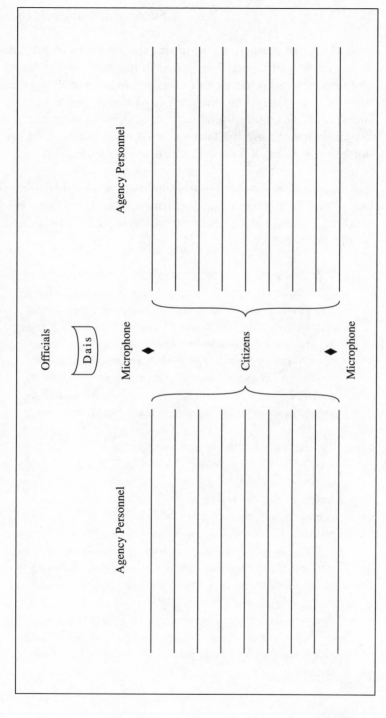

Figure 2.1. Typical Informational Meeting or Hearing Format.

One simple way to minimize the problem of presenters sitting or standing with their backs to the audience at an informational hearing is to move the decision makers from the center-front of the room to an angle off to one side (see Figure 2.2). Individual presenters then stand or sit sideways to them and the audience, giving the latter at least a partial view of everything that goes on. Of course, this is not possible if a raised dais is used.

No matter how diligently a conscientious presenter tries to mitigate the problem, the main drawback of an informational meeting is this we/they atmosphere that it creates, as illustrated by the following incident.

> *The state parks commission staff set up the hearing room in the common format — commission on a raised dais, staff and public below — the format they had used hundreds of times before. The purpose of the meeting was for staff people to provide information to the commission about options for new campgrounds. The ponderous and formal meeting process moved ahead for an hour or so, slowly fulfilling the stated purpose, until the commission chair realized that an unusually large number of citizens had filled up every empty seat in the room. After discreet inquiry of the staff, he was told that a contingent of people had traveled nearly 100 miles to be at the meeting, hoping that even though it was advertised as strictly informational, they would be allowed to testify about their community's concern for one of the park sites being considered. They had not tried to disrupt the proceedings, but they were obviously getting restless.*
>
> *The chair called a short recess to consider the matter with his fellow commissioners but without consulting staff. When the commissioners again took their seats on the dais, he acknowledged the audience by announcing that he was changing the purpose of the meeting. They had heard "enough canned information," he said in a benevolent manner, and now were opening up the meeting for a half-hour's public comment.*

Figure 2.2. Improved Informational Meeting or Hearing Format.

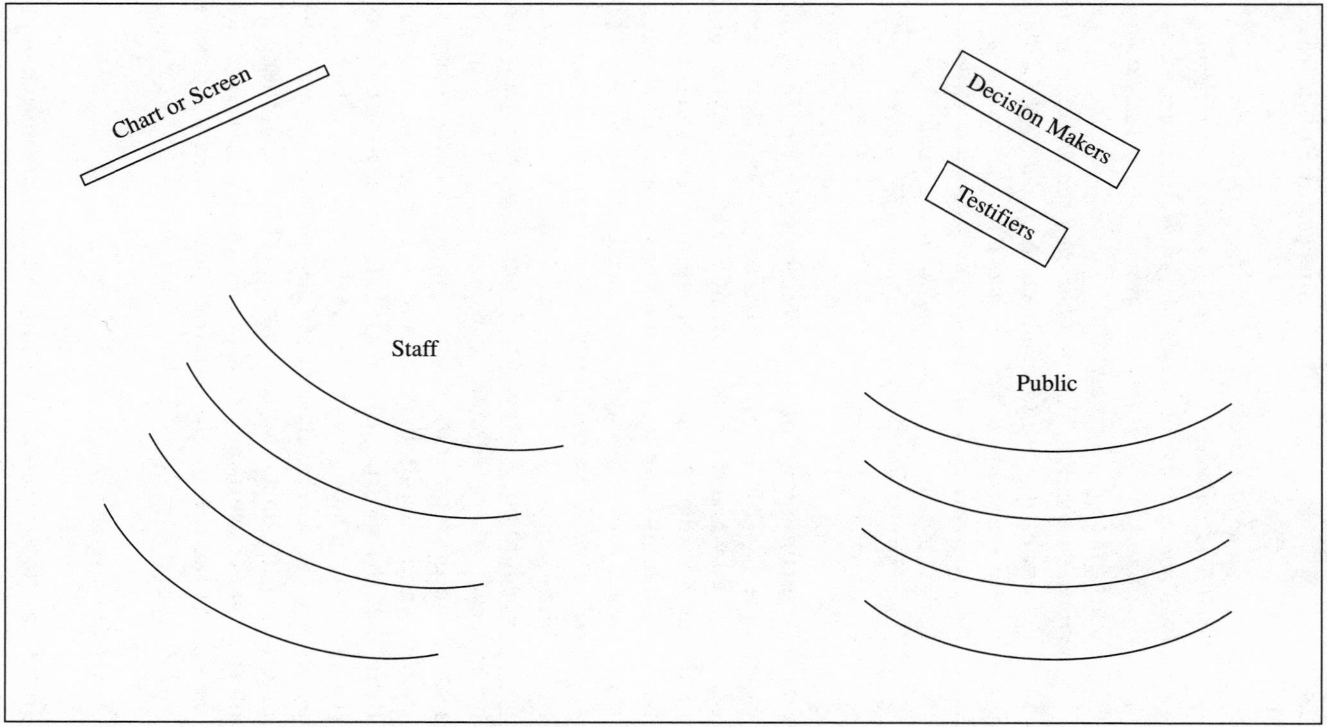

The first citizen stood up. Ignoring the chair's re-
quest to identify herself, she launched into a tirade against
the commission for showing slides of their community that
the citizens could not see from their seats. A second person
interrupted her, asking why the public was given only thirty
minutes to presents its views while "staff has hours." When
the meeting degenerated into a shouting match, the chair
saw no other way out than to gavel it to adjournment. As
the angry citizens shuffled out, some pausing at the door
to argue with staff, the chair and his fellow commissioners
shook their heads. "See what happens when we try to get
a little citizen involvement? We'll never do that again."

Unfortunately, they learned the wrong lesson from the experience. Citizen involvement was not the culprit. Difficulties occurred when the chair abruptly tried to convert an informational meeting into an advisory or problem-solving meeting without changing the format. The physical configuration was adequate for the initial staff informational presentation but inappropriate when the commission suddenly switched to soliciting public opinion. Some in the audience were seated behind posts and could not see the entire commission; others could not hear, because there were no microphones; and without a recognized procedure for participation, anxious citizens resorted to shouting and waving their arms to be recognized. No wonder, then, that the meeting disintegrated. When the chair decided to change to an advisory mode, he should at the very least have adjourned the formal part of the session and moved the commission off the dais onto the same level as the audience. With more advance warning, staff people might have been able to reconvene the meeting in a room more suited to constructive dialogue.

Panel Discussions

In the panel discussion, a variation of the one-on-one approach to presenting information, there are several presenters rather than one, each with a discrete message to convey. They are usually seated on a raised platform facing an audience. The panel is an effective way to give equal attention to different aspects of a subject and invite controlled audience interaction. The decision makers or primary receivers may sit off to one side, in the front row, or among the public. To denote their special status, they may be given time to respond or ask questions before the general audience can participate. Verbatim notes are rarely taken, though speakers may provide written transcripts of their remarks.

The success of the panel discussion format in generating information depends on the skill of the moderator to move matters along and the ability of discussants to communicate. (See Chapter Five for details.)

Advisory Meetings

As the middle ground between meetings that are primarily informational and those convened to solve problems, advisory meetings allow agency staff members or others to present information in a public forum and invite nonbinding advice on alternatives or a particular course of action. Thus there is a structured two-way dialogue.

Advisory meetings fail when the public misunderstands their limitations and develops unreasonable expectations of how citizens can influence the ultimate decision. The chair must present the ground rules at the beginning, telling the public how the results of this meeting will be used in the decision-making process.

> *The state transportation director, warned by her alert staff that citizens might think that they were to make the decision about the controversial issue under discussion, wisely decided to be forthright as she called the public meeting to order. "As most of you know, the transportation commission has the legal responsibility to decide the location of the highway bypass, but we've called this meeting in advance of their meeting next month to hear from you. Where do you think the bypass should go, and why? We're keeping*

a written record of everything you say tonight, and that record
will be available to the commission before they make a de-
cision. It's been our experience that they consider citizen com-
ments seriously, so what you say tonight is very important."
Valuable comments that influenced the ultimate decision were
heard and duly recorded, but it was clear and accepted by
everyone who the decision makers were.

All advisory meetings should begin with a presentation
of basic information, and either the talking head or panel discussion format is suitable. The workshop structure discussed
in the following problem-solving section can be modified to elicit
public opinion as well. Better still, however, is the community
fair, a unique format that reaches out to and receives comments
from an informed cross section of the public in a two-way process
of interaction and dialogue.

Sometimes called an open house, the community fair is
designed to allow maximum participation by many citizens, provide ready access to technical information, and solicit public
oral and written comments that are considered seriously by the
sponsors before they make a decision. The format is uniquely
suited to large-scale controversial projects, such as a comprehensive community plan or transportation alternatives, where
a considerable amount of technical information must be conveyed to an audience with diverse interests and needs.

The community fair is oriented to the citizen rather than
to the sponsor. It is a refreshing alternative to the typical public informational or advisory meeting, at which technicians and
professionals go to considerable length to convey information
and data, usually by giving overly long and detailed oral presentations to an increasingly restless audience.

As Figure 2.3 illustrates, the community fair requires a
large meeting room that can accommodate several activities simultaneously. School gymnasiums and cafeterias or church
meeting halls are generally the most suitable.

As people enter the fair, they stop by the information desk
to sign in and pick up an orientation packet, which includes
a small map and background material. Supplementing the map,

Figure 2.3. Advisory Meetings in Community Fair Format.

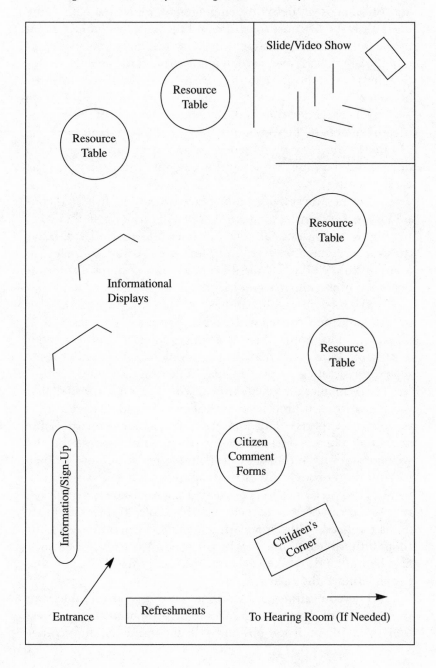

easy-to-read signs mark the different areas of activity. Staff and/or officials of the sponsoring agency, identified with name tags, T-shirts, or caps, roam around the hall, available to greet people and answer questions. Because the most effective community fair extends over several hours (from 2 to 9 P.M. is recommended), these hosts may take turns at shifts of two to three hours each.

The extended timespan is just one example of the citizen-friendly quality of the community fair. Seniors, students, retirees, or others who may be reluctant to go out at night can attend during the daytime, while working people can drop by in the early evening.

All the fair activities take place simultaneously and continuously. Citizens are encouraged to stay as long as they like, moving at an individual pace between informational displays (to examine maps, charts, and handouts), resource tables (to ask questions of the technical experts), and perhaps a continuously running informational slide show or video.

To accommodate families, the community fair should have a children's corner with coloring and story books and, if possible, some simple illustrative material on the subject under discussion. Child care may also be provided, along with simple refreshments such as punch, tea, coffee, and cookies.

To enhance the goal of two-way interaction, citizens should receive written summaries of technical data and be encouraged to quiz the experts about matters of particular concern. They should also be encouraged to give their opinions orally at the various stations and to fill out a simple questionnaire as they leave. Issues brought up during the individual discussions can be recorded on large sheets of butcher paper or newsprint tacked to walls or dividers near each resource table. If a formal hearing is required by the sponsoring agency, a separate section or room for oral testimony may be reserved. A court reporter may also be on hand to take verbatim testimony from citizens who cannot attend the hearing.

The community fair format requires considerable staff time: personnel have to organize; to be present to answer questions, provide information, and collect comments; and to analyze the comments after the event. The time is well spent, however. The very openness of this format—sending the message that the agency cares enough to meet the citizens on their own terms—creates a wellspring of positive community reaction. It also gives the agency the opportunity to obtain valuable advisory opinions on issues of importance.

> *Fifty thousand people spread out over two hundred miles in eight counties in two states were invited to participate, through several regional community fairs, in the planning process for a major river corridor that affected them all. The fairs were held in church meeting halls and school cafeterias from noon to 10 P.M. Citizens—many with their families— came at their leisure, milled around, met their neighbors, obtained information on issues of particular concern, and voiced their opinions. Even citizens opposed to the agency's proposal grudgingly admitted that they had been treated fairly and that they appreciated the agency's obvious efforts to meet them more than halfway.*

Problem-Solving Meetings

The purpose of a problem-solving meeting is to discuss a controversial issue and reach agreement on a solution that all or most participants can support. Those problem-solving public meetings that encourage participants to find areas of common agreement through consensus are less polarizing than those that make decisions by vote. Voting may be necessary, however, to provide closure on one issue so that the group can move on.

Every problem-solving meeting should begin with a summary of the information that all participants need to know. Many managers and directors make a common mistake that derails meetings at the outset: they assume that everyone agrees on what the issues are or they would not have bothered to come to the meeting in the first place. Acting on this erroneous notion, organizers call the meeting to order and then launch right into the discussion. To their dismay, they soon find that citizens know little or remember only selective information, depending on their varying experiences and prejudices. People may balk at discussing the problems that the sponsor has identified until they clear up ambiguities and misinformation or acquire what may seem to be elementary facts. Heated arguments and debates grounded on misinformation may prevent the meeting from ever getting to open and fair discussion.

To avoid these dangers, the managers and staff people who plan problem-solving meetings should structure the format so that the first part of the agenda is a short show-and-tell, giving everyone the same base of information. For a small group, a brief oral explanation followed by a limited time for questions from the audience suffices. Handouts that participants can read at their own pace are also helpful. For a large group — fifty or more — the goal can be accomplished more effectively with the addition of a slide show, video, or simple graphics. All information should be as free from bias as possible and be expressed in common, nonjargon terms.

If someone in the audience challenges the time spent on explanations ("Let's get on with the meeting. We've heard all this before!"), the chair may ask for a show of hands to indicate how many in the audience want to continue hearing the factual presentation. Usually the majority will vote to go on. If most people clearly indicate that they are sufficiently informed, skip the rest of the informational presentation and proceed to the discussion.

Problem-Solving Participants

The problem-solving meeting is the most complicated of the three types, involving multiple levels of communication: leader to group; group to leader; group to group; and individual members to each other. Keeping it all going requires strong and alert leadership: a quick-witted and alert chair, who acts as the catalyst and convener, and one or more facilitators, who channel the energy and knowledge of the group in positive directions. In particularly complex situations, the facilitator should have mediation or negotiating skills.

A third important participant — optional in the other types of meetings but essential in all problem-solving sessions — is the recorder. (See Chapter Two.) The recorder is the keeper of the group memory, performing the neutral function of getting down the essence of what the group is saying.

The recorder's writing must be in full view of the participants at all times. In a large group, an overhead transparency may be more readable than even the darkest marking pen on butcher paper or newsprint.

> *Public agency staff people were surprised that more than 100 people turned out to help them reach consensus on one of three options for development standards for a proposed recreational area. Prepared for just a handful of citizens, the agency director had brought only a chart pack and marking pens. Despite the large crowd, he plunged ahead with his prepared remarks, summarizing his salient points by writing on the chart with a colored pen that he had been assured was "friendly" blue. Friendly it was, but so light that it was unreadable to anyone past the third row. Some people sitting in the back of the room became quarrelsome and hostile. "Why are you writing so only the folks in front can see?" shouted one. "We're just as important as they are." "You're going to have to go over it again point by point. We want to know what you're writing," interrupted another. In a smart move that averted total rebellion, the director apologized and called a short recess until a staff member could find a black marking pen. He did have to start over, but at least he knew that this time everyone in the group could follow along.*

There would not have been even the potential for a citizen uprising if the agency had been more astute in its planning and had prepared overheads in advance. Ready for a large group, they could have shifted over easily to a chart and pen if only a small group had come. (See Chapter Eight, which covers audiovisuals.)

Problem-Solving Formats: The Workshop

For the discussion component of problem-solving public meetings of any size, given their purpose to involve all participants
in finding solutions to a public issue or developing a supportable program or plan of action, the workshop is the best general
format. (See Figure 2.4.) Though even well-run workshops appear formless to the unpracticed eye, they are successful only
if they are organized carefully and follow a specific timetable
and agenda. (As noted previously, a brief presentation of basic
information should precede the public discussion phase.)

Though problem-solving meetings are concerned with
serious topics, they need not take a heavy approach; in fact,
a light touch often works better.

> *The staff people of a parks and recreation district in a grow-
> ing suburban community were frustrated because one group
> of citizens harangued them for not being visionary enough
> to spend more on facilities while another wanted them to
> take a conservative, pay-as-you-go approach. Finally staff
> members brought both factions together, challenging them
> to come up with a spending plan that the majority could
> accept. After a staff presentation about the current situa-
> tion, the citizens were divided into groups of eight people
> each and given $5 million in "play money"—the annual
> amount that the district had to spend. Each group was then
> asked to agree on reasonable allocations that they thought
> would meet the community's needs. With this gaming ap-
> proach, which brought them down to the reality of having
> only a finite amount of money to "spend," participants be-
> gan to understand the trade-offs that agency staff members
> had to make. The group's final, reasoned consensus reflected
> everyone's heightened perception.*

If there are more than twelve attendees, individuals should
be assigned to smaller groups in order to have the participa-
tory interactive discussions that the workshop format requires.
Eight to twelve people at each table is optimal for small-group

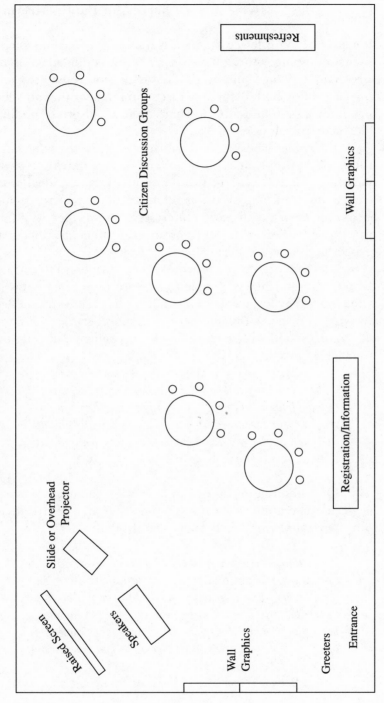

Figure 2.4. Problem-Solving Workshop Format.

discussions. With fewer than six it may not be easy to keep a discussion going; more than twelve, and it is difficult to make sure that everyone is involved. The small groups may convene as a large body both before the discussion to hear the introductory information and after to share their small-group findings and recommendations.

Everyone — speakers and audience — sits on the same physical level. Appropriate seating arrangements contribute to the dynamic, creative, synergistic environment that an ideal problem-solving workshop produces. Planners of the meeting should encourage people of disparate interests to sit together. With the proper facilitation, they learn from each other and begin to respect and accept differing points of view.

Meeting organizers must take an active hand to counter the natural tendency of people to sit with those they know or with whom they feel most comfortable. The easiest, most effective way to disperse the audience is by numbering each name tag to correspond with a discussion group and give the tags out in order as people sign in.

> *"John, according to the number on your name tag, you're at table four. Even though you're his wife, Mary, you can see that your tag says table five. Thanks for splitting up. We want to give you the chance to share your point of view with as many people as possible tonight."*

Once the reason for this system is explained, most people accept it readily, even though they may not be overjoyed to be separated from their friends and relatives.

> *The public meeting was called to discuss school taxes, a contentious issue in that particular part of the state, and the antis and pros were out in force. Most people accepted their table assignments when they were handed numbered name tags, but one of the more aggressive spokespeople complained. "Our side needs to sit together to put together our strategy," he admitted.*
> *"I understand," said the chair, firmly but with a*

smile, "but we want to give everyone a chance to speak with people who might not agree with them. You may even convince some of the opposition of your point of view." The complainer reluctantly sat down where he was told. After a particularly lively and creative discussion, he admitted that the "enemy" did not look nearly as fierce face to face.

Avoid using rectangular tables, especially in a large room that will have many discussions going on at once. People at one end may not be able to hear those at the other, nor can they maintain the personal eye contact and interaction important to good group dynamics. Round or even oblong tables facilitate a better discussion. Of the many reasons school cafeterias are desirable locations for public meetings (see Chapter Five), an important one is that they usually have round tables. If you have to settle for the oblong variety and acoustics are a problem, try to set up some groups in other rooms or even the hallway.

The discussion leader's seating choice also influences the dynamics of a problem-solving discussion. At a round table, wherever the leader sits becomes the "head." At an oblong table, discussion leaders maintain the best control by sitting at one end so that they can be seen and heard easily by everyone. Some egalitarian facilitators shun the authoritative stance and sit in the middle of the table. This puts them at a disadvantage, however: they have to keep turning their heads to and fro to acknowledge various members of the group. The recorder should sit next to the discussion leader so that they can confer as matters arise.

In a problem-solving workshop, there are many ways to encourage meaningful, productive discussion and help people reach conclusions or consensus. The appropriate method should be chosen in one of the first meeting-planning sessions, after you have agreed on the subject of the meeting and understand the knowledge and biases of the participants. A description of some of the more productive methods follows.

Brainstorming. An especially useful discussion technique, brainstorming protects shy members of a group from being bullied into submission by others more opinionated. It also gives a quick snapshot of everyone's central points of view.

The two ground rules of brainstorming are that everyone has a chance to say something and no idea is ridiculous or inappropriate. Going around the table, the discussion leader asks each party to say the first thing on this subject that comes to mind. Participants need not speak whole sentences; phrases or sentence fragments are acceptable, and sometimes even preferred. If there is considerable group energy, the leader may call for a second round of ideas, or even a third. The aim is to encourage all the new and creative thinking that the group is capable of without giving any loudmouth an opportunity to take over.

After all the ideas — the more, the better — are recorded, participants are encouraged to embellish or build upon others' suggestions. In further steps in the brainstorming process, the group winnows down the list, combines, discards, and finally agrees on a manageable set of goals, objectives, or action statements as required by the meeting agenda.

Reacting. Sometimes called the nominal group technique, reacting works well when the sponsors of the meeting first promulgate a set of principles or options that they ask a group to discuss. It is also a good technique by which to focus a heterogeneous group on a common objective. Participants are given pens and paper and asked to write down their highest-priority values, options, programs, or projects from among all those proposed by the sponsors. The facilitator then goes around the table and asks for everyone's first suggestion, second, and so on. This technique encourages people to do their own private thinking before participating in the group and structures the discussion, making it less likely to stray. More structured than brainstorming, it may lead to more specific conclusions. It also requires all members to participate — at least to the extent of reading from their lists — and may give them the incentive to defend their opinions later on.

Buzz Groups. In buzz groups, as in brainstorming, participants are asked to bring to the table as many ideas as they can think of; but in buzz groups, they are encouraged to ask questions or suggest issues that require clarification or further discussion from "experts." This technique works well when a relatively uninformed group needs to understand complicated issues before meaningful discussion can take place. The leader may say, "Let's record all your questions and the issues that you don't understand. Then we'll ask the resource people to explain."

Multiple Issue Stations. When several issues need to be addressed, each table can discuss a different one under the general umbrella of the subject at hand. A specialist for each issue serves as the technical or topical resource, aided by a facilitator and recorder. Participants move freely among the tables, staying as long as they wish; recorders keep a record of ongoing discussion and questions. This is only one step in the problem-solving process, however. After an hour or so of these intense discussions, participants convene in a large group to try to reach consensus.

Rotating Experts. As a substitute for a single informational presentation to one large audience, resource people can rotate among small groups, presenting their information to each one in turn. Intimate seating encourages people who might be intimidated by a large format to question the experts. Following each presentation, the small groups, guided by their facilitators, discuss the issues and reach consensus.

Whatever techniques are used, either singly or in combination, to stimulate small-group discussion, the facilitator must eventually ask the group to make choices or come to a conclusion. This step should be a natural outcome of the process of discussion. In one positive approach that does not polarize discussants, the facilitator summarizes on newsprint or large chart paper all the choices that the group has suggested and asks participants to talk about the advantages and disadvantages of each. If the discussion is framed in these terms rather than in absolutes of yes or no, even the most stubborn members of the group may see other points of view, making accommodation and consensus more likely: "We can all have something to say about advantages, even if we don't support a particular item," the facilitator can explain.

Another way to help the group make choices is to introduce some fun into the process. List all the options or alternatives on a large chart and give everyone a few colored stick-on dots with which to "vote" for their choices. People take this exercise very seriously and appreciate the anonymity that the dots give them. The dots tell the story quickly and clearly; the choices of the group are instantly recognizable.

If you want to gather additional opinions and test for concepts and ideas that people may have been reluctant to express verbally, ask all participants to complete a short questionnaire before they leave the meeting.

3

How to Publicize
the Meeting

Citizen-unfriendly notices are common roadblocks to successful public meetings. As to the common agency complaint that
the public does not come out to meetings because "people don't
care," they will care and they will come if they understand the
purpose of the meeting, how the outcome affects them, and the
role that they are expected to play in helping the agency reach
a decision.

Public agency managers cannot justify poorly written or
unclear notices on the grounds of statutory requirements for
content. Despite such requirements, they can direct their staff
members to use understandable, concise English, and even to
provide a translation into another language if the audience war-
rants it.

Before composing any meeting notice that will be deliv-
ered to the public, give thought to what people need to know
to be motivated to attend. This factor must take precedence over
what you think they should know or what you are required by
law to tell them. The information should be presented in the
general order given below.

Content and Format

- *Purpose of the meeting.* Citizens rightly become distressed if they show up at a meeting expecting an open session at which they can give testimony only to be told that only the staff and "expert witnesses" are allowed to speak. Similarly, the public will feel cheated if the notice leads people to believe that a definitive decision will be made before the meeting ends and they find out that the purpose of the meeting is to gather opinions for a later decision to be made behind closed doors. Managers must make sure that everyone participating in the meeting agrees on its purpose; then state that purpose accurately in the written notice. Experiment with attention-getting headlines: "Street-Widening Proposal" will encourage more citizens to read on than the bureaucratic "Notice for Potential Vacation of Certain Streets for Purposes of Accommodating Traffic."

    A council of governments in a growing metropolitan area was having trouble getting elected officials to attend a series of meetings titled "Urban Issues That Confront Us." When they sent out a notice announcing a "Summit Meeting to Solve Our Pressing Regional Problems," the attendance doubled.

- *Action to be taken.* What will happen as the result of this meeting? More meetings? Definite recommendations? A tax increase? Be clear and unambiguous.

- *Date, time, and place.* Do not bury this information somewhere toward the end of the notice; put it right up front. Recipients can thus consult their calendars and be spared having to read further if they are busy at the appointed time. On the other hand, with the purpose of the meeting stated so clearly and compellingly in the first paragraph, followed by the date, time, and place, they may decide to change their schedules because of the importance of the event.

- *Financial implications.* What, if anything, will the proposal under consideration cost? Will this street widening, annexation, park acquisition, solid-waste regulation, or other matter require the public to pay more money? Say so, and in terms that taxpayers can understand. Translate property-tax millage rates and other esoteric governmental jargon into increased taxes for a typical middle-class household or, if you are talking about sales or excise taxes, into so much per dollar of purchase.

- *Citizen participation.* Are ad hoc comments acceptable, or must people sign up in advance to testify? Can they register by mail? Is there a time limit? Failure to make all the rules clear in the notice may cause misunderstanding and hostility that will ruin the public meeting. If citizens accidentally or purposely misunderstand their role and insist, "No one told us that we have only three minutes apiece," the agency director can point out the clear, unambiguous statement to that effect in the invitation.

- *Optional additional explanatory material.* Attach simple maps or charts to illustrate complicated land-use or other matters. If there are several illustrations, employ consistent symbols such as crosshatching and gray-marked areas under consideration. Always include a north arrow and clearly mark streets or other familiar landmarks. Do not pass on a surveyor's dim pencil sketch annotated with scrawled notations that are impossible for laypeople to decipher.

- *Legal reference.* Include legal justification only if you must — preferably as an attachment that citizens can ignore if they wish without missing anything important.

Put all the above (with the exception of legal requirements, maps, and other extras) on one double-spaced page — two pages only if absolutely necessary. An outline such as that suggested above can be standardized for your agency or organization on the computer so that staff can just fill in the blanks. Remember to avoid verbosity and jargon. Give careful attention to format as well: wide margins, short paragraphs, and double-spaced text increase the likelihood that your notice will be read and taken seriously.

Audience

It does no good to have a readable notice if your mailing list is inadequate. How up-to-date is it? Failure to notify all citizens you are legally required to contact because of faulty record keeping, even if the blame lies with the assessor's or auditor's office, is indefensible. But it is almost equally important to communicate with those who are likely to be interested but whom you are not legally required to notify — neighbors who live farther away than the statutory distance, citizens who have shown a previous concern for the issue, community leaders, special-interest organizations. If the matter is controversial, you may be tempted to notify only those you are required to by law; but in the long run that is not good public practice.

Depending on the size of your agency and your community, you may need to keep several mailing lists, divided according to subject, known concerns or interests, geographical location, and other important factors. But people move and organizational leaders change. Be sure to update your lists at least annually. An effective way to keep track of peripatetic constituents is to mail your notices first-class, with a notation that you will pay the postage for any undelivered mail returned to your office. That service is more expensive than one-way, third-class mail, of course, but it pays dividends in happy constituents.

To reach a wide, somewhat undefined public not accessible through mailed notices, consider producing colorful posters — legal notices nailed to utility poles do not count! — that can be displayed at community and senior centers, shopping malls, and other places people congregate.

> *The city council was anxious that all the small community's citizens be apprised of an important open house to consider a proposed comprehensive land-use plan. On advice of staff, they invested $150 in a fifteen-foot banner and hung it on the outside of city hall, facing the most well-traveled street. Everyone who passed through town saw the sign, and many commented on it favorably when they came to the open house.*

Redundancy is an asset when you want to notify the public of an important meeting. These various methods are not mutually exclusive and should be used to their maximum effectiveness. Whichever method(s) you choose, try to keep your message light. As Exhibit 3.1 illustrates, taking a less serious tone

Exhibit 3.1. Sample Hearing Notification.

WE'RE COMING DOWN THE MOUNTAIN
FOR A
PUBLIC BRIEFING
ON THE NATIONAL FOREST ENVIRONMENTAL
IMPACT STATEMENT

*YOU AND OTHER MEMBERS OF YOUR
ORGANIZATION ARE INVITED TO ATTEND A
PRESENTATION WITH REPRESENTATIVES OF ALL
THOSE STUDYING THE PROPOSED DEVELOPMENT PLAN.
THEY WILL EXPLAIN THE OPTIONS, THE PROCESS
OF PREPARING THE ENVIRONMENTAL
IMPACT STATEMENT, AND THE
ROLE OF PUBLIC COMMENT.*

PLEASE JOIN US AT EITHER OR ALL OF THESE BRIEFINGS:

NOVEMBER 16   CHARLIE'S RESTAURANT, WINTERVALE

NOVEMBER 20   NATIONAL FOREST OFFICE

DECEMBER 6   ROOM A, CIVIC CENTER

ALL MEETINGS ARE BETWEEN 7:30 AND 9:30 P.M.
THEY ARE JOINTLY SPONSORED BY THE U.S. FOREST
SERVICE AND THE SKI RESORT.

---

can be an effective way to relay your message and still meet all the statutory requirements.

The words "We're coming down the mountain" set the right tone for this meeting on a controversial development issue; they indicate that the sponsors are willing to meet with people on their own turf. Note that one of the meeting locations is Charlie's Restaurant. The sponsoring agency balked when this nontraditional site was first proposed but accepted it when told by friendly citizens that it was the only common gathering place in this small community.

The following two exhibits illustrate all the points discussed in this chapter. Exhibit 3.2 is a notification form currently in use by a planning and zoning agency somewhere in the United States. A clearer, simpler, more citizen-friendly version of the same notice appears in Exhibit 3.3.

Exhibit 3.2. Traditional Notification Form.

Notice of Hearing to Rezone Property

Regarding Petition No. 1789222 PB, related to former Petition No. 5589167 PB, tax parcel 089507-214-576. The city is entertaining said petition from Thomas McIntire, owner of property at 2900 Elm Street, to rezone said property from RS-2, Single-Family Residential, to PS-1, Public Service.

The first public hearing on this petition will be held by the city's planning and zoning commission on February 28 at 6:30 P.M. in the third-floor auditorium of city hall. The second public hearing will be held by the planning and zoning commission on March 9 at 6:30 P.M. in the third-floor auditorium of city hall.

Following these public hearings, the planning and zoning commission will either vote to instruct the city attorney to draft a rezoning ordinance for this property, deny the petition, or continue the hearing in order to obtain additional comments and information.

The permitted uses for this property are single-family dwellings and customary accessory buildings incidental thereto. The permitted uses of the proposed zoning are libraries, senior and community centers, museums and art galleries, and public golf courses. Petitioner proposes to erect a senior or community center.

As a property owner within 400 feet of said property, you may make your views known to the planning and zoning commission by appearing in person at one or both of said hearings or writing a letter to be received on or before the date of the second hearing. Other citizens may also testify.

If you have any questions or desire to review this request in detail, contact the department of planning and zoning, city hall, room 725, or call 555-1155.

If this notice seems perfectly fine to you, step into the citizens' shoes for a moment. It fits all the legal requirements, to be sure, but it contains ambiguities, redundancies, and legalisms certain to confuse and perhaps antagonize the average person. The following revision, keeping all the salient points but written in lay language, is more likely to be understood.

Exhibit 3.3. Revised Notification Form.

Proposal to Change Use of Residential Property to Allow
Senior or Community Center   [*Attention-getting title*]

Thomas McIntire, living at 2900 Elm Street, has asked the city to rezone his property from residential use (RS-2) to PS-1, to allow construction of a senior or community center.   [*Purpose of the meeting*]

The city's planning and zoning commission may either allow or deny this request and is holding two public hearings to obtain citizen comments.   [*Action to be taken*]

Both hearings will be held in the third-floor city hall auditorium, February 28 and March 9, at 6:30 P.M.   [*Date, time, and place*]

If the property is approved as proposed, it will be used by a nonprofit corporation, which will not pay property taxes. The remaining property-tax-payers in the city will be required to make up the difference. The current property taxes paid on the property are approximately $1,500 per year.   [*Financial implications*]

All citizens who own property within 400 feet of this property are invited to testify in person or write to the department of planning and zoning before midnight of the second hearing, March 9. Any other interested parties may also participate in the hearing or in writing.   [*Citizen participation*]

For more information, contact Hortense Allen, project planner, department of planning and zoning, city hall, room 725, or call Ms. Allen at 555-5656.   [*Optional additional information*]

Please refer to accompanying map for specific site information. The legal petition for this case is on file as #1789222 PB and #5589167 PB.   [*Legal reference*]

In addition to being helpful to the public and setting the scene for productive and effective public meetings, clear and concise notifications have another value: they reduce the number of annoying phone calls to the agency from citizens who are not proficient in bureaucratic gobbledygook.

The first hint that citizens have of a public meeting is usually their written notice. Thus, as was noted earlier, it is counterproductive to use legal requirements as an excuse for being obscure or misleading. Agency directors should view such requirements as an opportunity to communicate clearly with their constituents and develop appropriate forms and procedures.

4

Creating the Right Environment
for the Meeting

It is 7:20 on a warm summer evening, ten minutes before the public meeting to discuss a proposal to widen a nearby freeway is scheduled to begin. Already a dozen citizens are milling around outside the high school. Behind the locked doors, frantic staff people hurriedly bustle about, trying to set up things in a gymnasium none of them has seen before. The agency manager realizes that she forgot to assign anyone to be in charge of registration, so she asks her assistant to set things up, directing him to a shoe box jammed with name tags, pencils, marking pens, and miscellany from their last public meeting. Two other staff people push together chairs and tables that were scattered throughout the room, another adjusts the slide projector and screen, while someone else searches for an electrical outlet for the coffee maker. The display charts fall down just as quickly as they are put up. To their chagrin, staff members realize that masking tape does not hold on concrete gym walls — but they do not have anything else.

Someone discovers that the projector bulb has burned out and hurriedly leaves by a side door to drive over to a nearby shopping mall, hoping to find a photography store still open.

The manager wipes her sweaty brow and looks up at the clock. "Okay, team, it's seven–twenty-nine. Ready or not, one more minute and we'd better let them in."

The crowd outside has grown. "This is a public building. They can't lock us out," one citizen is heard to grumble. When the assistant opens the door, people rush in, many hurrying by the registration table without picking up their name tags or explanatory material. The coffee pot is just beginning to perk, yet several people complain that it's just like this agency to serve a scalding drink when they should have had cold punch in the middle of summer.

At 7:45, everything is more or less ready—except that the slide projector now lacks both a bulb and an operator. The manager decides to begin anyway. "We're fifteen minutes late already," she says. "We'll just tell everyone that we've cut out the slides because we're starting so late. Okay, let's wing it."

And "wing it" they do—through the entire, awful evening. It is not until 10:30 that the last frustrated citizen straggles out and the exhausted public officials pack up to go home.

This meeting was programmed for disaster from the moment the agency manager and staff arrived—too late to cope with unfamiliar facilities and too rushed to handle inevitable last-minute problems such as the burned-out bulb. A seasoned manager might have been able to make a midcourse correction and hold a moderately successful session, but it would have been difficult given the environmental obstacles she and her staff created or confronted.

An important but often neglected key to the success of any public meeting is a positive, welcoming environment that sets the stage for the program that follows. The following specific factors require attention.

Satisfactory Site

Realtors are fond of saying that the three major factors that influence the marketability of a piece of property are location, location, and location. The same can be said of a successful public meeting. When planning your meeting, choose a site convenient and acceptable to the majority of attendees. What place is most well known and easily reached by the public you are inviting? Accessible to the elderly and handicapped? With adequate parking? Safe and well lighted?

Schools often meet these criteria. Most people are familiar with the location of their neighborhood or community schools and have a generally favorable, or at least neutral, feeling about them. Make sure, however, that there is ample seating for adults. Sitting for a half-hour in a primary school chair will upset even the most sanguine citizen.

Senior or community centers and church and synagogue meeting rooms — not religious sanctuaries, lest we are accused of mixing the secular with sacred — are also good for public meetings. They are usually in well-known, accessible locations and tend to have ample parking. A word of caution: acquaint yourself with the religious institutions in each neighborhood or community to be sensitive to any rivalries or interdenominational quarrels that would make some attendees uncomfortable and cause other people to stay away.

Senior and community centers, schools, and churches have other advantages as well. They usually have large, flexible rooms, ample tables and chairs, screens and microphones, and friendly and accommodating custodians — the latter are a real plus when and if anything goes wrong. The charges for using such facilities are minimal — a boon to public agencies, which cannot risk being accused of squandering public monies on fancy meeting halls. But do not let finances alone dictate your choice. Your local courthouse or city hall may be a cost-free site, for example, but neither would be an ideal location for a public meeting if the people affected live miles away and are averse to coming downtown.

Government facilities, such as hearing rooms or council chambers, present other problems. With a raised dais and fixed audience seating, they have a physical inflexibility and formality that discourage dynamic group interaction. This environment, which purposely encourages proper decorum and order at governmental meetings, is not conducive to the creativity and frankness necessary when citizens are called together to discuss, debate, or come to consensus on contentious public issues.

It is best to avoid private meeting rooms in banks or large businesses as well: these may be too upscale and intimidating for ordinary citizens. Hotels are the least favorable locations for effective public meetings, though they may have good parking. They either cost too much or give the aura of costing too much. When a nearby school or church is free (or nearly so), a public agency cannot risk being accused of wasting taxpayers' money by paying for a hotel conference room — even if the most expensive hotel in town is giving the agency a special price. In addition, hoteliers are in the hospitality, not the meeting, business. If they provide the room free, they will charge mightily for refreshments, microphones, screens, or any extras. Moreover, the partitions that separate large meeting areas into smaller units are usually flimsy and far from soundproof, and you cannot control who might be holding a meeting next door.

After a long search, the agency executive and staff chose a downtown hotel for their public meeting on proposed new environmental standards, because it was in a central location and citizens were expected to come from a large geographical area. Just as the meeting started, they were dismayed to hear band music coming out of the loudspeaker. The executive complained to the hotel manager, who just shrugged his shoulders. "Sorry, but that's no piped-in music. The steamfitters' union is having its annual dinner dance next door to you. But the band will take a break in an hour," he added.

Visible Signs

Even if you have chosen a well-known, accessible location, never assume that people will know where to go once they get there.

Always post large and visible directional signs in the parking area, on the outside of the building, by the entry door, and on the inside, pointing to the specific meeting room. Take extra cardboard arrows with you that you can place in the proper direction.

> *A state legislative committee holding a series of local hearings in a widespread geographical area chose nearby community colleges, because, as the chair insisted, "Everyone knows where they are." He was half-right. Everyone knew where the colleges were; but once there, especially at night, people were quickly lost. All the buildings looked alike; directional signs that were helpful to knowing students were confusing to unfamiliar citizens; and most parking areas were off-limits to visitors.*
>
> *Luckily, the manager whose staff organized these meetings made sure that these problems were solved ahead of time. Inspecting each site several weeks before, staff members noticed how visitor-unfriendly they were. Back at the office, they hand-lettered directional signs and arrows and mounted them at all the entry points, marking a clear route to the meeting room. The invitations included a small map of the campus and indicated where guest parking was allowed. Each meeting got off to a good start when several participants thanked staff members for making it so easy to get there.*

Convenient Timing

You must also avoid the common error of scheduling a public meeting for the convenience of the sponsors rather than the audience. It may be customary to conduct official business on weekdays from 8 A.M. to 5 P.M., but those hours are not convenient for a public meeting for any but the retired or the most committed citizen. Choose the time for your public meeting when most of the public can attend—7 or 7:30 on a weekday evening is best, although a weekend morning or afternoon sometimes works. Know the mores and customs of your community or audience and plan accordingly.

In one midsize city, some innovative community leaders in a predominantly Catholic neighborhood hold successful community forums from 9 A.M. to 4 P.M. on Saturdays. They find that citizens in this area are less tired and distracted then than during the work week and are willing to give up part of their weekends to discuss important civic issues. However, a meeting called on a Saturday in a primarily Jewish or Seventh Day Adventist community would bomb, because Saturday is the Sabbath for these groups. Likewise, in some communities Wednesday night is church night. Though not everyone is at Bible study or choir rehearsal, those who are not stay close to home.

Welcome Refreshments

Refreshments are a hospitable touch that have put many a potentially contentious meeting on a civilized track. A pleasant conviviality ensues when people have the opportunity to chat over a cup of hot coffee or tea or, on a particularly warm evening, a cold glass of punch. If the facility itself cannot make refreshments available, check out a local caterer or reasonably priced delivery beverage service. Though not mandatory, cookies are a nice addition. They can often be obtained as a donation from a nearby bakery or supermarket if you give the donor recognition on the program or post a small, tasteful notice on the table.

The citizens who came to discuss Department of Ecology plans to change the course of a nearby stream gathered in small, friendly groups around the refreshment table. Then someone noticed that styrofoam cups were being used for the beverages. The subject of banning such nonbiodegradable items in public places was a hot community topic just then, so many citizens boycotted the refreshments, loudly denouncing their hosts for not being more sensitive to the environment. The department supervisor vainly pleaded innocence; someone had merely ordered the service from the catering company. Failure to consider an important community value canceled out any of the pluses that the agency might have derived from the refreshments.

Room with a View

You have chosen the proper external environment. The location, date, and time are acceptable to most, and there is ample parking. You have set a convivial atmosphere with simple refreshments. All to the good.

The next concern is the room itself. It must be suitable in size and arrangement to further the goals of the meeting. First decide what you want to accomplish and then choose the setting that helps you meet your aims. What is the purpose of the meeting: to impart information only? To receive information only? To impart and receive information? To discuss issues? To solve problems? To reach consensus or a decision? To build goodwill? The wrong setup may create an environment that makes it impossible—or at least very difficult—to attain your objectives.

The sloped floors and fixed seats of a college lecture hall, for example, work well when there is one expert (the professor) and less learned but captive receivers (the students). On the other hand, it is a deadly configuration for any meeting at which public interaction is desired. If you are holding such a meeting at a college, choose a room with movable seats and a single level.

All meeting rooms should have the following features:

- Size adequate for the number of people expected—but able to be enlarged or divided if more or fewer attend.
- As little distance as possible between presenters and audience.
- Good acoustics and sight lines so that all attendees can hear and see with ease.
- Comfortable chairs and tables—but not so cushy that citizens can fall asleep.
- Adequate usable wall space for posters, charts, maps, and other explanatory materials.
- Ample nearby restrooms.
- Atmosphere that encourages a creative and cordial exchange.

City engineers had come several miles out of town to a newly annexed area to talk with the citizens about a controversial sewer construction project. Expecting much public interest, they had scheduled six meetings on different evenings in high school gymnasiums — big barnlike rooms whose most favorable attributes were accessibility and cheapness. At the first meeting, to the department supervisor's chagrin, there was a disappointing turnout: just four citizens came, outnumbered by the six city personnel. If the supervisor had insisted on keeping to the setup they had planned — auditorium-style seating with the engineers at the head of the room — they would have spoken to rows of empty chairs. Instead, he directed that they move two folding tables together in the front of the room and invited the people to join them.

After a short consultation, staff members agreed to abbreviate the length of their presentations and answer questions as they went along. When the seating configuration was changed and bureaucrats and citizens could see eye to eye, the environment changed — from suspicious and wary to friendly and cordial. In fact, this meeting was more successful than most of the more well-attended ones that followed. Citizens generated many creative ideas that staff members used in their final recommendations.

Size flexibility works both ways, of course. What if you plan a meeting for 25 people and 250 show up? Be prepared! Whenever possible, make sure that everyone has a seat, even if you have to drag in chairs from other rooms — still another good reason to use a school or church. Citizens will be good-humored about a little crowding as long as they can see and hear.

Consider using libraries, media centers, and similar facilities when you know that the subject of the meeting will attract strong-minded advocates. Carpeted floors, book-lined walls, and comfortable, living-room-type chairs tone down the rhetoric of even the most dedicated rabble-rousers.

The staff committee assigned to set up the room for the first economic development advisory committee drove up to the neighborhood school early and began to unload charts and graphs. The accommodating school maintenance man unlocked the front door and showed them to the room that had

*been reserved for them next to the gymnasium. "I hope that
the music won't bother you too much," he said. "What music?"
asked the startled coordinator. "Why, the 450-voice church
choir that rehearses in the gym every Wednesday night." The
coordinator exclaimed, "No one told us about them." "Well,
I guess no one asked," answered the maintenance man. The
coordinator thought quickly. There was no way to change
the meeting time or place; people would begin arriving at
the school in ninety minutes. But the school had many other
available rooms, so they were able to move the meeting to
the media center on the other side of the building. The ex-
uberant 450-voice choir could still be heard, but the sound
was muffled. The chair laughingly used the unexpected situation as an icebreaker at the beginning of the meeting.*

Necessary Name Tags

Most of us do not remember names well, and name tags are
an easy if unimaginative way to help us out. But test them out
before you buy, and use only those that can be removed easily.
Some sticky-backed name tags can pull off bits of fabric and
may justifiably anger users. Banks and utilities often provide
name tags free — printed with their logos, of course. If you want
staff and elected officials to be easily recognizable, give them
different-colored name tags. If you prefer that they not stand
out from the general public, have them wear the same color as
everyone else. Make sure that all attendees receive name tags
as they sign in. If you see people slip into the room without one,
seek them out and ask them to wear a name tag even if they
protest. In meetings where it is important to distribute people
randomly, name tags can serve a dual purpose: they can be
prenumbered so that people are automatically assigned to sit
at the numbered table that matches their name tag.

Fail-Safe Equipment

Provide pencils and pads at any meeting at which citizens are
likely to want to write anything down, and take care that your

audiovisual equipment does what it is expected to do. As we saw at the beginning of this chapter, such seemingly inconsequential matters as a lack of spare projector bulbs can upset an entire agenda.

Well before the audience arrives, test all your equipment — slides, overheads, videos, microphones — in the room in which you will be holding the meeting. If the public-address system has feedback or other problems, find the maintenance person or ask someone on your staff to help. A dress rehearsal of your slides or overheads in your office causes a false sense of security. Have another rehearsal in the room that you will be using; do not tempt the gremlins who lie in wait for trusting managers and staff members and cause havoc and distress when people are least able to cope. If the facility is not equipped with a screen, chalkboard, easels, working microphone, and podium, rent or bring your own. If you have to lay a cord across the floor, make sure that you tape it down so that you do not create a hazard.

Every director of an agency that plans or participates in public meetings should have a come-to-your-aid kit that is replenished after every meeting. At the minimum, include:

- Extra projector bulbs
- Extension cords
- Chalk, marking pens for paper, and marking pens for plastic boards
- Name tags
- Several varieties of tape
- Pencils, pens, and writing pads
- Scissors
- Aspirin
- More than enough copies of agendas and other handouts

No environment is ideal. Now that you know the importance of environment to the effectiveness of public meetings, choose the best available and take the time and effort to minimize or neutralize any negative effects or problems.

5

Making Effective Presentations

Will your meeting be congenial or confrontational? Comfortable or combative? Constructive or contentious? Does your agency really value citizen opinion, or is the meeting just window dressing for decisions that have already been made? Whatever the meeting's purpose, well-organized and -presented remarks set the proper tone for a productive meeting.

Few presenters are born golden-tongued orators, but everyone can learn effective presenting skills. The rewards of a good performance, of knowing that you have reached out and spoken to the concerns of your audience, are immediate and satisfying. The reverse can be said of a mediocre or poor performance: you know, and the audience knows, and no one is satisfied.

Individual Presentations

The steps discussed below can be used by any busy professional faced with making an individual presentation. They presuppose — rightly, in most cases — that you have a wealth of information at your fingertips. Your challenge is knowing what and how much to say to this particular audience. Most public officials know more than most citizens about sewers, environmental protection, land use, social policy, transportation, parks, and any number of issues that engage their professional time and attention. And most audiences — elected or appointed officials as well as the lay public — need to know far less than the professionals, even when they make decisions. Each audience requires certain information at that time and that place, and your job as a presenter is to figure out what that is and give it to them — no more and no less.

Remember Your Purpose

The first step in organizing any presentation for a public meeting is to decide what information the listeners need to know. That decision depends in large part on the purpose of the meeting: is it informational, advisory, or decision making? If, for example, some matter is up for discussion before the planning commission, the presentation should discuss options and/or a staff recommendation to help that body reach a decision. On the other hand, if the meeting is with a neighborhood and for advisory purposes only, the information should be presented in a more general and open way.

Know Your Audience

Organize your material only after you are sure of your purpose and have these answers about the audience:

- Number of people expected
- Average age and gender
- Occupation(s)
- General knowledge of subject
- Common opinions or biases
- Specific focus or special interests
- Known opposition to or support of the issues under discussion

Remember that the attention span of the average American adult is two and one-half minutes — and decreasing all the time. If your presentation is more than twenty minutes long, break up the monotony by choosing several speakers, using visuals to explain salient or difficult points, and scheduling time for questions to make sure that you deal with the issues in which the audience is most interested.

In an early planning session, after you have decided the general areas of information that will be covered at the meeting, choose the most appropriate and credible spokespeople: those who can best convey this information to this audience. As discussed in Chapter One, on leadership, every meeting must have a convener or chair: someone who is indisputably in charge. If you are speaking to an organized group, its president or leader takes that responsibility. At your own meetings, the agency director or a political leader such as the mayor should take that role. These people are not expected to have definitive information about the subject at hand. Their primary responsibilities are to keep order and to obtain and retain the respect and attention of the audience.

Similarly, as conveyers of information, the presenters do not have to possess the skills of the chair. They must, however, be able to convert complex or technical data into terms that a lay audience will understand. Audiovisuals can help, and there are a great variety from which to choose (see Chapter Six). But even the best audiovisuals cannot cover up the mistakes of a poor presenter.

Many city managers and bureau chiefs insist on making the major presentation at public meetings in the mistaken belief that only they have the appropriate credibility or status. Alas, as their staff people can attest after having to pick up the pieces, the top echelon may be the last people qualified for this task. Most often they are able generalists, not specialists; as such, they rarely know the fine points of the issues under discussion. It is best to leave the technical presentations to the professionals — insisting, of course, that they excise the jargon from their speech when talking to lay audiences.

> *The city manager knew that the proposal to widen the arterial street by removing fifty-year-old trees would be controversial, so he asked the city's traffic engineering consultant to*

*make the presentation at the public meeting, held at a local
school. After being introduced, the consultant immediately
darkened the room, turned on the slide projector, and began
to speak in a flat voice. Never varying his tone, he took
more than two hours to present all his slides, many of which
were redundant, although he did show sound mitigation
measures that could reverse the effects of the tree removal.
There were about seventy-five people at the beginning of the
meeting. After an hour, they began to slip out; and when the
consultant finished, only fifteen citizens were left. When
the city manager called for public discussion and questions
and there were none, he mistakenly surmised that the expert's presentation had mollified the opposition. On the contrary, they had been bored into submission — but only tem-
porarily. The next day angry citizens petitioned the city for
a special meeting — not to hear any more information, they
insisted, but to be heard themselves on this important issue.
The consultant's presentation, while technically sound, was
inappropriately long and tedious, and it unnecessarily alien-
ated an important audience.*

Organize

Every presentation should contain no more than three major
points. Professionals and technical experts often protest this important rule; they insist that they have thirteen points, even thirty, and
that the audience must be apprised of all of them. But no audience
is all-inclusive; each has its own special interests. In light of the
above example of the street widening, consider my earlier ad-
monition to organize presentations around what each particular
audience needs to know: the adjacent neighborhood has different
concerns than downtown businesspeople, who have different interests than senior citizens or the planning commission, and so
on. By considering the audience first and adjusting your remarks
to its needs, you can indeed find the three major points that interest these people. If the issue is a construction project, always
include a time schedule, even if it is subject to change. That is
the piece of information that citizens most often want to know
and public officials most often want to avoid discussing.

After defining your audience and its needs, you may find that one presenter cannot cover all the material. If so, bring in others — but not any more than necessary, lest you risk repetition. Three presenters is usually a sufficient number: the first to give the introductory or broad perspective; the second, details; the third, more information or a summary. Each presenter should also be available to answer audience questions.

Build bridges with the audience with words such as *we, our,* and *us* rather than creating a gulf with *you* and *your.* It is important that citizens believe that you care about the issues as much as they do, even though you may disagree on specific points.

Help your listeners keep track of your presentation by using connectors such as these: "I'm going to cover three points today. The first is . . . ," "Next, let's talk about . . . ," and so on; or, "That's one way to look at the issue. On the other hand . . . ." Summarize at the end by repeating the most important points you want people to remember.

Use commonly understood short words and phrases and direct nouns and verbs. If you must use jargon, explain it or provide a handout with a glossary.

Avoid jokes and humor directed at particular ethnic, racial, religious, or other interest groups. Such disrespect can be politically and personally damaging. On the other hand, do not be so stilted and formal that you cover up your genuine warmth and humanness. While public officials usually make poor stand-up comedians, they endear themselves to audiences when they tuck in appropriate anecdotes about themselves and their families and colleagues or appeal to people's pride and sense of fair play.

> *The local police chief began his remarks at a crowded neighborhood meeting by acknowledging his and the participants' shared concerns. "I understand your neighborhood's concern about adequate traffic control. My ten-year-old son crosses Logan Boulevard every day to go to school, and in our neighborhood we parents formed a safety patrol to try to slow down traffic in the morning." Later he commented, "We've all watched our city grow, and I'm proud that so far we've been able to work together to solve the tough issues."*

Never write your presentation word for word or you will read it word for word and sound mechanical and insincere, no matter how much you practice. It is better to outline your remarks, using visuals such as charts or graphs to help people follow along and to understand difficult concepts. Divide your presentation into a discernible introduction (what you are going to say, lightened up with an anecdote or two), body (those three cogent points we discussed earlier), and conclusion or summary (action or further steps needed). Keep the presentation short enough to fit easily into the time allotted.

Practice Until Perfect

It is important that time to practice be part of the premeeting planning schedule. After all the presenters have outlined their separate remarks, get everyone together and rehearse. If possible, include other staff members who know the audience or the subject but are not presenters. Despite your individual busy schedules, try to have at least two rehearsals: one several days before the meeting so that you have time to change the text or visuals and a dress rehearsal a day or a few hours before. Find time at a long coffee break, during a brown-bag lunch, before or after work — whenever everyone can get together. The only way you can be sure that all the important points are being covered, that no one is running over schedule, and that repetition has been eliminated is to take the time for these dry runs. If the meeting room is unfamiliar, at least one person should visit it and report back before you rehearse. It is important to rehearse even if you are making a presentation in a familiar environment, however. Even when you know the setup, you still need to practice who is saying what when, where you should stand or sit, and the best place for your audiovisuals.

During your rehearsal, talk about what each of you will wear. This is not at all frivolous. People generally form their opinions about strangers in the first thirty seconds — before anyone says anything. Posture, demeanor, and dress are important nonverbal signals, and you want to send the right ones.

County engineers sponsored a series of meetings to talk to low- and moderate-income residents about a sewer system that the state environmental agency required the county to install within the next ten years. The engineers were aware that this was not a popular subject, because the new sewer would raise everyone's property taxes. The meetings were for information only; citizens could not change the mandate. They could, however, express their opinions about the process.

After the engineers rehearsed their remarks, they discussed what they should wear. They started by asking themselves what the particular audience expected county engineers to look like. They agreed that the dark suits, white shirts, and subdued ties that were standard dress for a meeting with downtown businesspeople were too formal and intimidating for an evening meeting in the suburbs. On the other hand, they felt that open-necked sport shirts and slacks would give the impression that they were too casual about such a serious subject. They decided rightly to wear sport coats, ties, and slacks. These engineers were all men, but women should have had the same concerns and chosen suits or tailored dresses — no pants and no frills.

Deal with Stage Fright

Even with the most meticulous preparation, most of us have some symptoms of stage fright before a presentation. Sweaty palms? Keep one hand in your pocket and out of mischief, but make sure that you have no keys or coins that you can jingle. The audience will never know that you have sticky hands or a perspiring forehead unless you give it away by wiping profusely. Dry throat? Avoid coffee, tea, colas, and other caffeine-laden beverages for several hours before; slake your thirst instead with cold water. Squeaky voice? Citizens who have never seen you before have not heard your normal voice, so never apologize. Memory loss? Take a drink of cold water (always keep a glass nearby), readjust your notes, look over the audience knowingly, and repeat what you just said for added emphasis. If all else fails and you still forget what comes next, summarize and finish up. The audience will never complain that your presentation was too short.

The key points to remember about stage fright are that nearly everyone has some of it sometimes, audience members cannot tell that you are nervous unless you tell or show them, and knowing your material and practicing will give you the confidence to overcome the worst of it.

Another way to give you added assurance to deal with stage fright is to arrive at the meeting early. As was noted in other chapters, there are untold details at a public meeting that can go wrong. You walk in at the last minute at your peril. Being early gives you time to set up your audiovisuals, adjust the microphone to the height and audio level you require, find and use the bathroom, and become as comfortable as possible with the particular features of the room. Being early has another advantage: you can meet and greet the public as people arrive. Much as you may prefer to run and hide from perceived enemies or critics, it is better to disarm them by being at the door to shake their hands, engage in small talk, and make it clear that you respect them and will be cordial and polite—whatever your differences. Building rapport with as many people as possible will give you unexpected friends and convince others to give you the benefit of the doubt if matters become contentious. Keeping yourself busy will also deter you from becoming nervous and tinkering with, and probably spoiling, your well-organized and rehearsed presentation.

Panel Presentations

Panel presentations, which allow for diversity of attitudes and expertise, can be very effective. The key players are the panelists and the moderator.

Role of the Panelists

If you are a panelist at a public meeting, the same general rules apply to preparing and giving your remarks as apply when you are the sole speaker. Choose remarks appropriate to the audience, be organized, speak from notes instead of a prepared script, and adhere to the time schedule. Never be the one for whom the warning bell tolls — especially more than once. In addition, make sure that you know the following before organizing your panel speech: your specific topic, time allotted for each presenter, order and format, where you are to sit, and other logistics.

If you have a choice of position, volunteer to be either first or last. If you are a skillful lead speaker, your presentation can provide the framework for the entire discussion and, in effect, cause the others to respond. If you are last, you can be the summarizer and synthesizer — the one whose remarks are most likely to be remembered.

Role of the Moderator

The unheralded moderators, who must guide, organize, and stimulate the thinking of the group without revealing their opinions or prejudices, are essential to the success of panel discussions.

Deal with Panelists. The care and feeding of participants is the moderators' major responsibility. They arrange for any audio-visual equipment and an operator, if necessary, make sure that there are sufficient handouts, test the microphones, provide drinking water, make sure that the temperature and lighting in the room are comfortable and that canned music is turned off, and do everything possible to make the presenters and audience comfortable.

Some moderators are given the additional responsibility of choosing the participants on the panel. Giving due attention to gender, race, political affiliation, and other factors important to the issue and to the audience, moderators should choose participants who represent a variety of interests concerned with the subject under discussion.

Effective moderators make every effort to confer with all the participants well before the day of the meeting, briefing them on all the matters discussed above and encouraging them to summarize their remarks from careful notes rather than read ponderous written documents. If a meeting of the entire panel is

not possible, the moderator should arrange a conference telephone call so that everyone can review each other's outlines and
note redundancies or gaps. The quality of the discussion is en-
hanced when everyone has the opportunity to rehearse and or-
chestrate needed changes beforehand.

> *"Listening to Florence just now, Jack, it sounds as if you're*
> *both saying the same thing, but no one is covering the issue*
> *of financing. Will you do that instead?" Or, "According*
> *to your summaries, you sound as if you all agree with each*
> *other, but the audience will want to know the differences.*
> *Who wants to take the opposite point of view?"*

The moderator should obtain a short biographical résumé
of each participant and make interesting, informative introduc-
tions that add credibility to each speaker.

Although everyone should come early, the moderator
should be the first on the scene to check out the room and equipment, leaving ample time to take care of those last-minute problems that are sure to arise.

Make People Comfortable. As noted in Chapter Four, the seating arrangement has a significant effect on the quality of any
meeting. Arrange the chairs to facilitate discussion. For small
groups — those of twenty-five or fewer, including panelists — try
chairs in a U-shape (with panelists seated at a table at the open
end) or around one large table. An auditorium or classroom
style, with the audience facing the presenters in the front of the
room, is most common for a larger group, but it somewhat in-
hibits free exchange. Arrive early to rearrange things to suit
your purposes.

Place identification cards in front of the panelists that spell
their name and affiliation correctly in bold black ink. The cards
need to be large enough to be seen by everyone in the audience.

Do not skimp when ordering microphones. It is essential
that all members of a large audience be able to hear all the
speakers. Two people can usually share one tabletop mike comfortably, but three definitely make an awkward crowd. In a
small, informal setting, panelists may sit down when making

their set remarks, though it is generally better to have them stand before a microphone and podium. They may sit when answering questions.

Moderators make presentations too — albeit brief. In their opening remarks, they should welcome everyone; inform the audience where the bathrooms and telephones are located; review the purpose of the meeting, issues to be discussed, and schedule, including breaks and time for questions; and ask the audience to hold questions and comments until all the presentations have been made.

To avoid distracting bobbing and weaving, moderators should introduce themselves and all the panelists at the outset, stating names, credentials or affiliations, and general topics. Then panelists can give their prepared remarks in turn without further introduction, following one another in the order in which they are sitting.

It is important to provide means for everyone in the audience, including those reticent to speak aloud, to ask questions.

> *After the conclusion of the panel presentations on the subject of U.S./Japanese sister-city relationships, the moderator asked for questions from the audience. Several Americans stood up, but after a few minutes it became obvious that none of the Asian guests were asking questions or commenting, even though they had been specifically invited to participate. The puzzled moderator called a short break and conferred with one of the Asian panelists, who informed him that Japanese were not accustomed to speaking out at public meetings. She suggested, however, that they might respond if written questions were invited. After the break, the moderator handed out cards, inviting audience members to write out their questions anonymously. He noted some of the Asian guests nodding and smiling. Soon afterward, several questions, some obviously from the Asian point of view, were submitted.*

Keep on Time. Moderators may give someone else the job of watching the clock, but they must not hesitate to cut off a presentation that is running well over its allotted time. Using a prearranged hand signal such as a wave or thumbs-down, politely but firmly signal the speaker when the time is up. Stand up to give your message emphasis. If the speaker ignores your non-verbal sign and continues, with no end in sight, get tough. Stand near or at the microphone and say, for example, "Betty, I'm sorry, but I see by the clock that your ten minutes are over. I know that you wouldn't want to cut into Bob's time." If for some reason you are nervous about controlling run-off-at-the-mouth speakers, bring along a loud alarm or timer and use it.

Even if the meeting is running on time, the moderator must be sensitive to the audience. If people are fidgeting, dozing off, talking to their neighbors, or showing other signs of boredom, call an unscheduled two-minute break or stretch-in-place.

The moderator is in charge during the question-and-answer period and should be prepared to start the discussion by asking a question of each participant or by "planting" questions among friends or colleagues in the audience. If you are in a large room, there should be extra microphones for use by the audience.

Decide in advance whether it is necessary to ask questioners to state their name and affiliation and enforce whatever rule you make. There is no one correct way. If the proceedings are being recorded, it is probably important to know everyone's identity. On the other hand, if the meeting is general and it does not make any difference who is speaking, do not bother with names: more people will be willing to participate if they can be somewhat anonymous. Accept only one question per person unless everyone has had a turn and there is time left.

Every public meeting should begin with one or more informational presentations, and every presentation needs to be carefully organized and crafted if it is to set the stage for the discussion that follows. Presenters, panelists, and moderators all play significant roles in assuring the success of public meetings.

Answering Questions

Except on very formal occasions, most elected public officials usually set aside time after their speeches for questions, and for very good reasons. First, if the question-and-answer period is handled well, speakers have an opportunity to reaffirm their message. Second, they engender audience goodwill by giving people the opportunity to clear up ambiguities or uncertainties or state their own points of view. A well-structured question-and-answer session can go far in cementing the bonds of mutual understanding and respect that the presenters created with their original remarks.

If the question-and-answer time is disorganized, however, or if the speaker is rude, unprepared, or on the defensive, the good relations previously established with the audience are jeopardized. It is important to prepare as seriously for the Q-and-A period as you do for your presentation. Making it the subject of one of your premeeting planning sessions, review the composition and expectations of your audience and list the ten most challenging questions people are likely to ask. If your planning group is not sure, consult with others who know the audience and its concerns. Then rehearse short, succinct answers to each question. To your subsequent surprise and delight, you will find that audiences rarely ask more difficult questions than you can devise.

> *State transportation department engineers held three public meetings to discuss a proposal to widen a heavily traveled street from two to four lanes. Starting with the same basic information, they tailored their remarks to each specific audience. The downtown businesspeople who made up the first group were interested in how the construction would affect access to their establishments as well as how much it would cost each of them. The next audience, older residents at a senior community center, wanted to know about how to limit speeding on the street and whether the proposal would raise property taxes. The third, a preschool parents' group, was concerned primarily about children's safety but also about taxes. Knowing these concerns, the transportation engineers rehearsed questions that each group would be likely to ask, preparing themselves with financial information and a construction time schedule for the businesspeople, statistics about speeding for the seniors, and so on. Forearmed, they were*

*able to answer all the citizens' questions and concerns and
to appear credible and competent to each group.*

Choose the Actors

Decide the following matters beforehand so that you are as organized for the Q-and-A as you are for your initial presentations. Who will call on the questioners? Answer most of the questions? Handle rude or unruly people? End the meeting? These
roles should be assigned on the basis of ability, not because of
hierarchical status. A strong chair can keep control of the meeting by fielding all the questions and assigning the most knowl-
edgeable person to answer them, for example, while a chair who
is more of a figurehead should take a backseat and let the facilitator or presenter take charge.

It is important to prepare the audience beforehand by announcing when you will take questions—preferably after all the
prepared remarks have been made. Send nonverbal signals to
indicate a willingness to meet the audience on its terms and your
interest in whatever concerns people. If you have been speaking behind a podium, walk away for questions. If you have been
on a platform, move to the floor. If you are tied to the umbili-
cal cord of a stationary microphone, make sure that it has a long
cord. A clip-on mike gives you more flexibility.

Answer Each Question

Listen carefully to each question, nodding to indicate your at-
tentiveness. You do not have to agree with what everyone says,
but you must always respect each individual. Help the rest of
the audience hear or understand fully by repeating or paraphrasing each query.

Be direct and honest, but take a tip from successful politicians: do not fall for "red herrings" or baited questions. When
someone says, "You just repeated the same old stuff that your
staff report says. When are you going to get to the issues we're
interested in?" you might answer, "If you'd like to see us include
other items, we'd be glad to hear about them later; but first,
as you can see by the agenda, we've promised to answer questions about the content of the report as you've heard it."

Answer generically and avoid holding a conversation on an issue specific to only one individual or situation: "Please see me later to talk about our time schedule for construction on your street. But if the rest of you are interested, I'll take a minute to explain all the details that the state considers when we put together our construction schedules."

Generally avoid put-downs such as a brief yes, no, or maybe. Sometimes, however, one of these responses may be just the right answer to a long-winded question that is clearly out of bounds and annoying the audience as much as you.

Move off the bureaucratic pedestal by relating your answers to the audience: "Yes, I know how hard it is to know what's going on at city hall when we're open only when you're working. Let's see a show of hands. How many would come to an evening hearing?"

Show that you have been listening by agreeing with points that others have made. Never argue. Maintain your poise and composure despite the slings and arrows of discontented citizens and deal with contentious people with courtesy: "Well, ma'am, I understand your concern, but we'll just have to agree to disagree on this one."

Humor is a good way to relieve stress or tension, but only if it is in good taste and directed to the speaker, not the audience. Never tell a shopworn or offensive joke.

Some people come to public meetings just to make a statement. Hear them out, waiting patiently until they take a breath, which even the most long-winded surely will. Then cut in immediately: "Thank you. I see by the hands that many other people have questions to ask. Let's call on the man way in back." Avoid someone close to the first speaker, because he may be a buddy who will back him up. Impatient people risk losing the audience's goodwill if they try to force everyone to ask a question. Do not challenge a questioner unnecessarily by retorting impatiently, "Now that you've stated your opinion, will you please give us your question, sir?"

Be aware of and control your body language and nonverbal behavior. If you scowl while saying, "Yes, I understand," you contradict your words and appear insincere.

Never try to run away from a difficult question by referring it to staff or known experts in the audience unless you have their permission beforehand. At the very least, you risk further embarrassment for yourself as well as for the experts if they do not know the answer. On the other hand, do not hesitate to say that you do not know; then offer to obtain the answer as soon as possible. Ask questioners to give you their name, address, and phone number after the meeting. Do not waste everyone's time taking down that information during the meeting.

End on Time

If you greeted people before the meeting and maintained an open and receptive demeanor when you made your presentation, you can take comfort in knowing that most of the audience is either neutral or on your side, unless you give people reason to turn against you by being rude and thoughtless during the Q-and-A period. Given the chance, an audience will often discipline its own rowdy members: "Come on, Phil, sit down. The rest of us want to hear what they have to say."

Stop the Q-and-A period three to five minutes before the scheduled conclusion so that the chair or facilitator can make a quick summary. This is one of the most neglected but most important parts of any presentation. You, your staff, and the audience have been together for a while now, and people have most likely forgotten some or all of your major points. Tie things together before you adjourn: "We certainly have enjoyed being with you these last two hours. In summary, we would like to leave you with these three points: [the most important things you want them to remember]. Thank you."

6

Using Audiovisuals

It is generally accepted that people remember 20 percent of what they hear, 30 percent of what they see, and 50 percent of what they see and hear. Audiovisuals can help you increase the retention capability of your audience, but only if they are prepared carefully and used appropriately.

Too many managers allow staff members to rely on audiovisuals as the primary means of conveying their message rather than using them for what they do best — supplement and reinforce verbal information. Nothing can take the place of the most effective messenger — the human being who is prepared, articulate, and attuned to the audience. Even the best audiovisuals, by their very inanimate nature, are second best. In fact, the wrong audiovisuals — or the speaker's use of the right audiovisuals at the wrong time — can hinder the effectiveness of the best-prepared presentation.

It was 7:30 on a warm spring evening. The thirty-five physicians, nurses, administrators, and citizen activists on the health futures advisory committee were eager to hear the

*consultant's remarks. He had been brought to town at con-
siderable expense to give them the latest news of health care
trends around the country. Committee members were looking forward to talking with him about models that they could
adapt to their community's health care delivery system.*

*Mr. Outside Expert was all business when he came
to the podium; unloading a sheaf of papers from his brief-
case, he asked that someone dim the lights. "I know that
you can't see this, but . . . ," he began, and proceeded to
prove himself right. He clicked on an overhead projector and
showed the first of many single-spaced, tightly printed pages
from a book — his book! He soon made it very clear that
all he had to say about health care he had already written.
Assuming that no one in the audience had read his book,
he proceeded to read whole paragraphs projected on the
screen — page after page after page. When Mr. Outside Expert was finally through with his reading lesson, the audience was half-asleep and too numb to ask but a few cur-
sory questions. As they filed out, disappointed committee
members agreed that everyone's time and money would have
been better spent if they had just purchased thirty-five of
his books and asked Mr. Outside Expert to stay home.*

Many of us have endured — worse yet, some of us have
perpetrated — such misuse of audiovisual equipment. However,
proper audiovisuals properly used can help you show and tell
difficult technical information and arouse and maintain the interest of your audience. Most people today are accustomed to
obtaining most of their information from the media, which distill it into thirty- or sixty-second TV or radio announcements
and terse newspaper headlines accompanied by short stories and
simple illustrations. We may bemoan the effect of all this on
the American public's understanding of complex issues, but we
would do well to master these techniques if we want to make
successful presentations.

Graphs and charts that clearly illustrate technical concepts
and processes or numerical comparisons can help a lay audience
follow a complicated oral presentation and become the base-

line for everyone's understanding and discussion. They have yet
another value: in a contentious or controversial situation, skilled
speakers can focus hostile questions on the graphics and explanatory material, thus directing anger and confusion away from
themselves and toward a neutral entity.

Instead of using audiovisuals only at the beginning of a
presentation, as people tend to do, interject them midway as
well, when the audience is getting sleepy or inattentive. There,
they can help the speaker sum up the main points in a presentation or reinforce the audience's understanding of key points.
Used again at the end, they can make sure that everyone is still
on track.

It takes real skill to be a humorous speaker without demeaning or poking fun at the audience, but a clever visual at
the right time can do the job for you.

> *A professional city planner in a major West Coast city in-
> tersperses his presentations with overhead transparencies of
> cartoons that illustrate situations familiar to planners and
> lay audiences. This technique has more than once defused
> a tense situation. As the audience smiles or laughs at the
> common foibles they see on the screen, they become more at
> ease with each other. The speaker is no less professional
> for showing that he does not take himself or his profession
> too seriously.*

Audiovisuals can also save time. Spoken words can be
abbreviated by illustrations if they are simple and clear. They
should never be crammed so tightly with information that they
themselves need lengthy explanation, however.

No One Fits All

It stands to reason that no single audiovisual technique suits
every situation, and yet many people act as if it can. Staff members may become protective of slides or an expensive video, for
example, and overuse them or use them inappropriately. Managers should not allow people to use an audiovisual simply be-

cause someone has invested time or money putting it together for another purpose. At the premeeting planning sessions, after you know the content of your presentations, choose your audiovisuals by evaluating them in terms of these factors:

- *Purpose.* As noted above, audiovisuals should complement, not overwhelm, your message. What is your reason for using them at this particular meeting? Would this audience be impressed with something slick and spendy, or are these people more likely to find your message credible with a down-home and casual approach? There is a great variety, as you will see in the pages that follow.
- *Size of audience.* Chalkboards and charts have limited viewing range and thus do not communicate messages well to audiences of fifty or more; likewise, slides and movies may overwhelm a small group.
- *Visibility.* More than one speaker has set up the paraphernalia for a slide show only to realize too late that a third of the audience will be sitting behind pillars or posts without a clear view. Arrive early and position the screen, posters, or charts. Then move through the room to check visibility. If visuals cannot be seen easily from all the seats, move the chairs or move your material, redo the visuals, or—if you are unable to change things adequately—go on without them. Audiences are forgiving if you explain why you have to give just an oral presentation, but they are unforgiving, and sometimes downright hostile, if all or most of them cannot see the illustrative materials.
- *Budget.* During your planning sessions, decide what budget you need and how much money you can spend, and then choose the audiovisuals that meet those criteria. Clever graphic artists with more time than money can do wonders. But the cost definitely goes up, and the quality may go down, if you ask them to bail you out at the last minute.
- *Presenter's skill.* Never use an audiovisual that is too complicated for the speaker to handle with ease. Hold a dress rehearsal that includes all the charts or boards and practice standing to one side, not in front of them, when writing or

pointing. Write legibly; if even your best handwriting is unreadable, enlist a helper to write for you, or have the writing done by a graphic artist ahead of time. If you know that you are apt to be especially nervous or are a klutz with even the most simple slide projector or video recorder, bring an assistant who can tinker quickly and successfully with balky machinery.

- *Message.* Suit the medium to the message, not the other way around.

The Audiovisual Menu

The most commonly used audiovisuals are presented alphabetically in the pages that follow. The discussion of each includes usage tips, advantages, and disadvantages.

Audiovisual	Advantages	Disadvantages	Usage Tips
1. Butcher Paper	Inexpensive, portable, and disposable. May be preprinted with information the speaker wants to cover or used effectively to record ideas as they are expressed by either large or small groups. May be rolled up and taken back to the office for retyping in permanent form.	May appear too impermanent and frivolous for some formal occasions, such as hearings.	Always write firmly and clearly with dark-colored pens—no yellows, greens, or oranges. Check out the host-site beforehand. More than one presenter with a roll of preprinted butcher-paper charts and a box of tacks has been thwarted by an adamant hotel manager who would not allow any holes in her expensive wall coverings. Masking tape sometimes can be used; find out the rules of the establishment well in advance so that you are not caught unaware. *Not having ascertained the rules beforehand, the public works director reluctantly admitted to a large audience, "We have these charts we want to show you but the hotel manager won't let us tack them on the walls. I'm sorry I didn't bring any tape. Can I have two volunteers to hold them up for me? We only have a dozen or so." Finding volunteers the same approximate height was one problem; getting them to hold their arms up for an hour without collapsing was another.*

Audiovisual	Advantages	Disadvantages	Usage Tips
2. Chalkboards or Whiteboards	Free if they come with the territory, as they usually do in schools and meeting or convention centers. Flexibility is the primary asset as words or ideas can be changed with the flick of an eraser or erasing fluid.	Not always available — particularly in hotel or chuch meeting rooms — and nearly impossible to rent or take with you. Clumsy. Impermanent; you will have to erase your previous words or arrange for a quick transcription if you run out of space. Limited visibility, especially white chalk on a scratched, dull, much-used surface. Most schools still have old-fashioned chalk- or black-boards and old-fashioned chalk, but too many of the boards are worn-out and therefore hard to read. The school-room and pedagogical memories they evoke may be positive or negative, depending on your presentation skills and the background of the audience.	Whiteboards much better than chalk-boards — they are easier to read — but be sure you have the right kind of marker. Do not rely on your hosts to provide any equipment — not even marking pens. *Facilitating a workshop with elected officials whom she wanted to impress, the consultant picked up the colored pen that lay next to the whiteboard without looking at it closely. After she had written several lines, she attempted to erase her text and was embarrassed to find that she could not. She had grabbed the wrong pen — it was not "dry ink," the only suitable ink for whiteboards. This simple but obvious mistake made it much tougher for her to gain the confidence of the audience when she imparted her message.*

Audiovisual	Advantages	Disadvantages	Usage Tips
3. Flip Charts	Inexpensive, portable; you can easily bring your own rather than borrow one from the host-site. Press-on letters may be used to enhance neatness and legibility. Ideas may be written down neatly beforehand and then referred to as you speak of them. Like butcher paper, flip charts can convey your openness to new ideas and may encourage spontaneity and creativity, because they allow you to jot down ideas that arise from you or your audience.	Because they are so handy, flip charts are often misused. May not be seen clearly by the audience unless you use bold, strong, primary colors. Avoid yellow, which tends to fade out, and magenta, which people either love or hate. Small, scrawly writing also can be a visibility problem; if you cannot write legibly, have someone else do it, or practice until you can. For ease of viewing in the typical room, letters should be at least two inches high. Not a good visual aid in a large room. Check out the host-site. If the flip chart cannot be seen easily from the back row, flip over to something else.	Clutter is the enemy of flip-chart literacy, mainly because we expect too much from this medium. Write ideas or fragments, not complete sentences. But be sure to discuss or at least mention everything on the chart. If you skip over or ignore several points, you tempt the audience to fill in the blanks on its own, and the answers may not be the same as yours.

Audiovisual	Advantages	Disadvantages	Usage Tips
4. Graphs, Maps, Diagrams, and Charts	Portable and flexible, if made beforehand on heavy, good-quality paper or posterboard that does not bend, tear, or wrinkle easily. More expensive than flimsy butcher paper or flip charts, but also more permanent.	Spoiled by the instant messages of the modern media, the attention span of most viewers is extremely limited, while at the same time, they expect high quality. Crowding in too many details and mediocre to poor lettering or duplication are pervasive problems. Too often done by technical experts without concern for the limited understanding of lay audiences.	Always check them out in the room in which they will be used, or, at the very least, know the size of the space and apportion them appropriately. Do not stint on quality of materials. Use bold colors. Make sure there is a surface to which they can be attached, or bring your own easels or room dividers.

The city manager wanted good graphics for a series of budget presentations he was going to make throughout the community. To save time and money, he had his staff prepare only one set of illustrations and took it everywhere. Unfortunately, this approach was effective only some of the time. In some settings, such as grade school classrooms, the charts were too large and clumsy; in others, such as downtown church meeting halls, they were too small. The credibility of the message and of the presenter suffered in both cases.

With the availability of computer software programs for graphics, too many people who cannot draw a straight line think they can now be artists. Not so. The same rules for clarity, boldness, and simplicity apply as when we are all in the dark ages of pen and paper. Do not load your graphs, maps, diagrams, and charts with so much text that they require many minutes of observation or explanation. It is particularly important that your illustrations be self explanatory if they are viewed by an audience that is meandering about. Simple but complete legends or titles are matters typically overlooked. Every map or photograph of a geographical area must have a north arrow; always include a standard title block that includes the name of the agency, department, the preparer (if an architectural or engineering firm, for example), and indication if this is part of a series ("Transportation Alternative 1, 2, 3, and so on"). If there is any chance that the managers of the facility will not let you mount the material on a wall, bring your own easels.

Audiovisual	Advantages	Disadvantages	Usage Tips
5. Handouts	Help to avoid ambiguity or misunderstandings because you have something tangible to put in the hands of each member of the audience. Appropriate for: • outline of your presentation • important points you want people to remember • copies of material you are projecting in overheads or slides • charts, diagrams, and checklists • articles from newspapers or magazines • bibliography or related references • glossary of technical terms	Primarily, sloppy preparation. In this era of state-of-the-art duplicating equipment, it is inexcusable to hand out anything that is messy or difficult to read. If your copying machine has broken down at the eleventh hour, take your material to a 24-hour commercial copier. If you cannot rectify the problem, leave the handouts back at the office and make do without them.	There are two kinds: those you use as reference when you are speaking and those you want the audience to read later. Both must be prepared with careful attention to: 1) format: use outlines, lists, and short paragraphs; 2) attribution: make sure all material is printed on your agency's or department's official stationery, or with the source neatly typed in one corner; 3) date and title: this is a pervasive omission, as obvious as it seems; 4) numbered pages: another common mistake is to leave pages unnumbered, probably because they were assembled from a variety of sources at the last minute; 5) quality of reproduction. Never give handouts to the audience beforehand, or you will be rewarded by seeing the audience, heads down, reading the material, instead of heads up, listening to your explanation. Distribute each handout just before you are going to use it. Do not insult the group by reading every word; instead, paraphrase and amplify the ideas on the written page. If your material is for reference only and you are not using it during your presentation, have it ready to be picked up afterwards. Always have enough so that each member of the audience can have one or more. If you run out, offer to mail copies to those you have slighted.

Audiovisual	Advantages	Disadvantages	Usage Tips
6. Microphones	Permit speakers to project their voices without strain and thus to speak with ease to an audience of any size. Many people are not familiar with microphones and thus shy away from them when they should be used. If you are going to give many major presentations, learn how to speak into, regulate, and be thoroughly comfortable with the device.	As with anything else that aids your presentation, microphones can be a handicap if you are not familiar with them in general or if the one you are using is of inferior quality, emitting squeaks and static.	A microphone is a very sensitive instrument; it will pick up and amplify whispers and asides, coughs, and paper shuffling—sounds you may not want the audience to hear. Nothing aggravates an audience more than being expected to read the lips of the speaker, however. If you cannot be heard well throughout the room, use a microphone. Test the mike beforehand. Never give the audience the impression that you are an amateur by waiting until everyone is seated and then banging on the mike forcibly to ask, "Can you folks back there hear?" Learn how to use the instrument just as you practice with any other audiovisual technique. Know how to turn it off and on. Adjust it to your height beforehand or take the time to adjust it just before you speak. If you move around during your presentation, ask for a clip-on microphone. If none is available, stay put.

Audiovisual	Advantages	Disadvantages	Usage Tips
7. Models	Most people do not understand drawings or maps with the same ease as the engineers or planners who produce them. A three-dimensional, scaled-down version of proposed buildings, highways, or any major changes to the landscape can be very effective. Citizens can walk around the model and get some sense of what the finished product will look like. A good model can be the centerpiece of an interesting oral presentation.	Expense is a substantial negative factor. Good models can cost thousands of dollars and require an expertise not usually found among professional or technical staff. Inflexibility is another disadvantage; once you have invested in an expensive model, there is often little you can do to make changes short of ordering another one. Depending on the size of the model, portability may be limited. Another disadvantage is the flip side of one of its main advantages: only a limited number of people can view a model at one time.	Encourage citizen participation by investing in miniature moveable buildings, trees, cars, and other components so that people can see the results of various options. Mark streets and other landmarks clearly and distinctly.

Audiovisual	Advantages	Disadvantages	Usage Tips
8. Posters	Portable and easy to mount, dismount, and remount; good posters can present the essence of a message simply and effectively.	May be moderately expensive if you have to hire outside artists or pay for printing a large quantity. Cannot communicate a complicated message, and may be considered too frivolous a medium for a serious subject.	Be careful not to expect too much. Best as a vehicle for slogans ("Don't trash it . . . Recycle!") or bold, simple photographs or drawings.

Audiovisual	Advantages	Disadvantages	Usage Tips
9. Projected Media: Overheads and Transparencies	Simple to prepare, do not require extraordinary artistic talent or technical know-how. Inexpensive transparencies can be made easily by drawing on ordinary paper with a felt marker; computer drawings or more complicated illustrations can be reproduced on an office photocopier. Transparencies are flexible; you can change the order to suit the needs of specific presentations and uncover the information as you go along, thus controlling what the audience sees. You also can encourage audience participation by changing or erasing written text, or by starting with a blank transparency and recording people's ideas. Of all the projected media, overheads have two distinct advantages: you can face the audience when showing them, and they can be seen easily in both a slightly darkened room, or, better yet, normal lighting conditions. Projectors are portable, if somewhat bulky, and not too costly either to own or rent. You may use any light-colored, blank wall to project your image, though a screen is always best.	May be overused just because of their advantages. Avoid the tendency to project closely printed lines of text. Keep your message simple and unambiguous. Transparencies can become dog-eared if used too often, but are easily and inexpensively remounted or replaced. Typewritten sheets are not legible enough. Use all capital letters and triple spacing or larger print.	The most important investment you should make is in professional time to make projected media appealing and interesting. Never use anything with which you are not thoroughly familiar. An important caveat to remember: if anything can go wrong, it most likely will go wrong—from power failures to burned out light bulbs, missing or too-short extension cords. Never stand with your back to the audience and read the image on the screen. Never go on without checking your equipment in the room where you are giving your presentation. That will not ensure that no problems will arise as soon as your back is turned, but it will somewhat increase your chances of success.

Practice how to position your material so that you can do it with the least distraction to the audience. Use examples to which they can relate. "These are overheads of sketches I made of Dresden taken on my last trip to Europe. If you use your imagination think of what we could do in our city" may make an audience think about how we could afford such an expensive junket instead of what you would like them to do—get ideas they can transfer to their town. |

Audiovisual	Advantages	Disadvantages	Usage Tips
10. Slides	Can convey feelings and images and capture people's imagination. Suitable for all sizes of audiences, but especially effective with large groups.	Require a somewhat darkened room that invites the audience to doze, especially if the show is too long — 10 to 15 minutes is the optimal length. There are more bad slide shows than good ones as too many presenters use the medium to overwhelm their audiences with redundant and boring images. Fancy artwork and graphics can substantially increase the cost and perhaps give the wrong impression, as some audiences will question this "unnecessary expenditure of public funds."	Experiment in the room beforehand and turn off as few lights as you absolutely need. Err on the side of having too few slides rather than too many. All lists should be succinct phrases, not whole sentences, leaving it to the presenter or narrator to fill in the details. Look closely at any photographs you want to use. Are they clear? Appropriate? Do they advance your message? A slide show may be simple and inexpensive or glitzy and costly, have its own sound track or be accompanied by someone reading a script. If the latter, make sure you have a microphone that works and a speaker who reads well and has rehearsed the technique of simultaneously flipping pages and changing slides. Be careful not to overwhelm audience members with Hollywood-type productions; they will be distracted from your message by their concerns over where a public agency on a stringent budget found the money to pay for the show.
			Gremlins breed in slide shows and can cause all manner of havoc. Never use one that is unfamiliar to you. Even if you have shown the show many times, review it before each meeting unless you have locked it up in a vault between showings. Remember that slides go in the tray upside down and backwards.

Audiovisual	Advantages	Disadvantages	Usage Tips
11. Video and Films	Primary advantage can also be your downfall. In this age of sophisticated TV and movie images, most people are accustomed to getting most of their information and entertainment from the video or movie screen and readily accept this way of presenting ideas. The challenge for a public agency on a limited budget is how to compete in quality with the slick commercial productions to which your audience may be accustomed.	Cost and time are primary negative factors. Very few agencies can produce their own video or films and therefore must hire outside contractors.	Make sure the firm you hire can do more than put pretty images on the screen—it must know how to translate technical information into simple terms laypeople can understand. Large companies, especially utilities, may have video or movie studios they will let you use; some may donate their equipment or personnel and make the production for you. In all cases, make sure you control the content. If you write your own slide or video script, remember that people hear words differently than when they read them. The script should mimic common speech patterns: short, concrete words and relatively simple sentence structure. It is far better not to use this medium at all if you cannot do it right. If you have the resources, however, either one can be a very effective carrier of your message.

Principles of Audiovisual Use

- Use audiovisuals to enhance, not replace, your oral presentation.
- Choose the medium that will make your message more clear or meaningful to each audience.
- Make them simple and unambiguous. If you have a considerable amount of information to convey, use several charts or slides rather than cram too much into one.
- In all lists, use phrases rather than complete sentences.
- Utilize a size and scale that can be seen easily by everyone in the room.
- Choose strong colors — black or dark blue on white for charts, blues and greens for maps, with red or orange highlights on either.
- For projected media, paraphrase and augment written information; never duplicate pages from a text.
- Before turning on the slide projector, check and double-check to make sure that the slides are in the right order, the right way up, locked in place. Always test them out in the actual room as close to performance time as possible.
- Bring your own equipment, including spare light bulbs, extension cords, marking pens, masking tape, and other necessities.
- Keep the room as light as possible — dim but not dark — giving your audience no opportunity to doze off without being noticed.
- Distribute handouts only when you need to refer to them, or give them to the audience as they leave.
- Face the audience, not the chart or chalkboard. Practice until you can write sideways with ease.
- On charts, use a wood pencil, your finger, or an outspread hand as a pointer. Except on an overhead or slide, where a flashlight is more useful, a human appendage is more friendly and less pedantic than a mechanical instrument.
- Show only those visuals that you need at the moment. If necessary, have a helper remove your charts or graphs as you finish with them.

- If you have any doubt about whether you can be heard, use a microphone.
- If anything goes wrong, do not apologize or fiddle unduly with the machinery. You should know your subject well enough to extemporize when necessary.
- Remember that one picture is indeed worth a thousand words, but only if it is the right picture!

7

Dealing with
Meeting Participants

We are not surprised when politicians, managers and their staffs, and others who have a stake in the outcome of the meeting try to promote their own agenda. Neither should we be surprised when members of the public express points of view that are contrary or appear to challenge the leadership. Thoughtful, enthusiastic, and vocal attendees, even if they tend to get off the track that we have laid so carefully, should not be considered barriers to successful meetings. Chairpeople, facilitators, and discussion leaders are helped to deal with any problem situation if they maintain a sense of humor, show goodwill, have knowledge of specific discussion techniques, and adhere to the democratic process. For ease of reference, common and uncommon types of people, and ways to deal with them, are discussed alphabetically below.

Accusers. "I've been listening to you for twenty minutes now, and it's the same stuff you bureaucrats always say. You don't want to hear from us citizens. You'll just go and do what you want anyway." Accusers are often arguers gone amok. The first step in dealing effectively with them is to make sure that their accusations are not correct. If accusers are right, you have no recourse except to promise to mend your ways. If you have truth on your side, several techniques can diffuse accusers. Answer patiently, but not patronizingly, "Sir, I can understand your frustration; I've been to meetings like that too. But I can assure you that this time we're listening and will take everyone's comments into consideration." Then follow up your words with action: "Charles over there is tape recording everything being said at the meeting, and we'll go over the tapes afterward. If you want to add to your comments, please give us written suggestions before you leave." Diffuse the accuser's anger by requesting a positive contribution: "Let's review what we've discussed already. If we haven't included your concerns, you're welcome to restate them for us." Resist the impulse to answer in the same tone of voice. If accusers have been to many public meetings, they probably have some cause for skepticism.

Apathetics. "I'm not really interested in being here. My spouse [or boss or neighbor] nagged me, so I tagged along." Disgruntled apathetics do not have to say anything to reveal their feelings. Just watch their body language: they tilt back in the chair, arms across the chest in a show-me attitude, drum fingers on the table, fidget, and look everywhere but at the speaker or discussion leader. In a large gathering, this behavior and attitude affect only those immediately near the apathetics and can usually be ignored by the chair; not so in a small group, where they can disrupt the flow of discussion. Instead of allowing apathetics to sit outside the group (thus reinforcing their count-me-out attitude), welcome them into the circle: "I'm sure that we can make room for one more; it's important that we hear from everyone." Challenge their harmless but restless natures by engaging their interest: "Jill, you were in Costa Rica last year. How does their literacy rate compare to ours?" Or ask them to take on a neutral task that will get them involved: "Would you make sure that everyone turns in a questionnaire after our discussion?" If all efforts fail to engage them, keep a watchful eye out to make sure that their insidious virus does not affect others.

Apple-Polishers. Some folks have not changed since grade

school. Back then, they were always trying to be teacher's pet by giving the answer they thought was expected or jumping up to do favors. In the adult world, they still try hard to please the person in authority. Though they may have become more subtle, they give themselves away by their undiscriminating deference to the leader: "Joe's in charge, and as far as I'm concerned, whatever he says goes." Much as it may please your ego, that attitude puts too much of a burden on the leader and is not in the interest of good group dynamics. It is nice to be complimented on a new shirt or outfit, but on your shoes and haircut too? Be wary of fawning and false flattery and be suspicious of a possible hidden agenda. Answer the compliment with a simple thank-you and then keep things moving by directing a question to the entire group. Apple-polishers can be persistent, and they may make other members of the group feel hostile if they appear to be succeeding in gaining the leader's favor. If you do not succumb, you will earn the respect and gratitude of the group.

Arguers. Some of this type start out with a smile and a disarming, self-deprecating remark such as, "Well, I know this is only my opinion, but . . . ." That preface is the last time the arguer will be modest. If allowed to continued unchecked, arguers will make it clear that they value their right to state their point of view more than they want to hear from anyone else. They speak loudly and authoritatively from an arsenal overloaded with gossip, hearsay, innuendo, and sarcasm. Listen politely the first time, or even the second, lest you be accused of not giving them the respect they or the group think they deserve. But take control soon. Neither argue back nor ask a question that invites them to continue the discussion and discourages others from participating. Remember, it takes two to argue. Your reasoned response and fair-handedness will wear down the most determined arguer.

Attackers. A mentally or physically abusive bully may target the chair, a presenter, or even someone in the audience. If you, as a public official, are being attacked verbally, the old adage "Sticks and stones may break my bones but names will never harm me" may give you some comfort. Try not to take the assault personally. Attackers are most likely angry not at you but at the system, the agency you represent, or perhaps even a lazy-bum brother-in-law who works somewhere in the system. Attackers usually speak hurriedly and in a loud voice. Resist the tendency to answer in the same hostile tone and accusatory language. Put them off guard by slowing down the momentum and answering deliberately, in a modulated tone. Emphasize a particular point that you know has the concurrence of most of the group or will focus everyone's attention back on the agenda or the time schedule: "Yes, ma'am, it's obvious that you feel strongly about this issue, but it's already eight-thirty and we promised to finish the other three items on the agenda before we adjourn at nine. Why don't we take up everything else now, and we'd be glad to stay to talk with you afterward." Another effective technique for cooling off attackers and the heat that they generate is to call a short recess. Take that opportunity to confer with your colleagues or friendly members of the audience and involve them in a strategy for dealing with attackers and depriving them of their primary weapon: the us-versus-them ploy that pits the agency against the public. But avoid an ill-timed or overly long recess that allows attackers to marshal their forces and put you on the defensive. On rare occasions you or your staff may actually be attacked physically. If you are forewarned and the threat is serious, arrange for protection. Plainclothes guards are less intimidating to the audience than uniformed police, but if the uproar gets out of hand at the meeting, you may have to call the police anyway. Alternatively, you could adjourn the meeting; but realize that you are only deferring, not solving, the problem.

Some elected officials seem to enjoy verbally abusing staff members who are making oral presentations. If you are the hapless target and you want to keep your job, maintain your professional demeanor; do not fight back. Most likely you are the scapegoat for a political purpose — perhaps the official is trying to get reelected by pandering to a particular constituency — that has little or nothing to do with you personally.

Bashfuls. Truly bashful people have little self-confidence and do not believe that they have anything to contribute; thus they rarely volunteer their opinions. Do not embarrass such individuals by seeming to pick on or talk down to them: "Well, Jane, you've been quiet as a mouse all evening. Come on, now. What's your opinion?" A better way to bring them around is to invoke an inclusive process that involves the whole group. (This works best with no more than fifteen or twenty participants.) Go around the table and ask each one in turn to answer a specific question: "If you could think of one word to describe our community, what would it be?" Bashful types can thus participate without being singled out. Another way to involve them is by catering to their shy, retiring natures: appoint them recorders. They are often accurate, thoughtful, and articulate as long as they do not have to speak out loud.

Chip-on-the-Shoulders. People with a chip on their shoulder are habitually resentful and angry, daring everyone to insult or injure them wherever they go, not just at your meeting. Those who know them are wary or even hostile, and generally not very forbearing: "Come off it, Harry. No one said that you were at fault." As the leader, you can kill them with kindness instead. Give them credit for even the most insignificant contribution, implying that they have no excuse for acting like the injured party.

Dominators. There are two kinds of dominator: those who know nothing and just want to boss other people around and others who know too much and are impatient with any deliberative process. Their outward behavior is similar: they try to monopolize the discussion, present their opinions forcefully, and intimidate the more reticent members of the group. Dominators do not wait very long to show their colors. If you have seen them in action beforehand and find them a part of your group, head them off early: "I know that you have strong opinions about this, Stephanie. Why don't we start off by taking a minute for you to tell us what you think the issues are?" After she pontificates for her allotted time, you can cut her off with impunity by turning to others to respond. Though dominators seem to run on incessantly, they have to breathe eventually. When they stop to take that breath, be alert. Seize the opportunity to interrupt or redirect the discussion. If these benign methods fail, simply ignore the dominators. They are used to this treatment.

Doubters. "I don't see how this can work. It never has before." Doubters are incurable skeptics; they cannot bring themselves to believe that anything good can happen that they did
not personally observe or invent. They often accompany their
negative remarks by nonverbal behavior, such as scowling, knit-
ting their brow, or shaking their head vigorously. If they are
allowed to monopolize the discussion, they may influence others.
Take control by suggesting that the group first hear everyone's
ideas without discussion or evaluation. When doubters start their
down-in-the-mouth comments, you can refer to the rules: "Remember? We said that we wouldn't prejudge anything. Let's
hear what everyone thinks." Be positive: "I can understand why
you feel that way, but with all the good minds around this table,
I'm sure that we can figure out how to work out our problems."
After enough of this positive reinforcement, even dyed-in-the-
wool doubters will hear an idea that they can support.

Dropouts. Slumping in their seats in the back of the room
or off to the side, dropouts yawn, doodle, look out the window,
or conspicuously read something entirely irrelevant to the subject of the meeting. The leader needs to make a quick assessment about whether to try to win them over or ignore them.
Consider several factors: whether the dropouts always behave
this way or are bored just with this issue; whether their inat-
tention will infect the others; and whether they will have anything constructive to say if cajoled into being part of the group.
In other words, is it worth diverting time and attention from
the others to court them? The dropouts' negative attitudes are
often directed not toward you but toward the subject ("I thought
this meeting on zoning was a real estate seminar"), their com-
panions ("My friends made me come"), or even indigestion ("My
stomach hurts"). If there is a break, you may want to seek out
the dropouts to see if anything reasonable can be done to engage their attention. Benign neglect may be your best recourse,
however, because they are generally too lazy to convince others
to drop out with them.

Eager Beavers. Some people are so anxious to be liked and
to be part of the group, that they seize on any or all ideas with-

out giving them much thought. One might say, "I really agree with Joan. We should put all our money into a new park," only to back a completely contrary point of view just a few minutes later: "Wow, Jack's right! Let's spend all our money on a good, old-fashioned street fair." Eager beavers are too flighty to be good leaders, but they can be valuable at backing up whatever course of action the group embarks on. Hear them out politely, but do not expect them to be bellwethers.

Fence-Sitters. Like eager beavers, fence-sitters have few opinions of their own. They are reluctant to say anything, however, until they see where the majority, or the people with the most status or influence, are going. Fence-sitters figuratively — or sometimes literally — look to the right and to the left to see where the opinion wind is blowing before they commit themselves. They also equivocate: "It seems to me that Mary is right when she says that we need a budget increase, but Jerry is also right when he says that we need to rein in expenditures." Fence-sitters can contribute to a discussion when you need balance, but they are ineffective in a partisan argument and in helping the group come to a conclusion. It does no good to become impatient with them or try to force them to make a premature decision or recommendation. Do not expect them to leap off that fence until it suits them. You may have to ask the group to vote in order to force fence-sitters to make a decision.

Gossip-Spreaders. "Well, I didn't hear it firsthand, but . . . ." Gossip-spreaders enjoy the attention that they receive when they disrupt meetings with hearsay that has little or no basis in fact. Their voices sound authoritative, but their words are vague and indefinite. They throw out just enough information to tantalize people or stimulate their imaginations so that others are encouraged to add their own tidbits. If you think that someone else may have more or correct information, call for it: "Has anyone else heard the mayor say that he'll fire the city manager?" If no one can refute the gossip-spreader, but you know that the group is getting off track, enlist everyone in finding a solution. "Does anyone know how we can find out what's really going on?" Call a short break. If the gossip-spreader's snippet makes

no difference to the discussion, do not refer to it again when
you reconvene. Gossip-spreaders thrive on the fact that nearly
everyone enjoys talking about someone else.

Hair-Splitters. Usually accountants, attorneys, scientists,
or computer wizards who are well paid on the job to dissect data,
hair-splitters do not understand that the same positive attributes
that serve them well in their professions can discourage free-
flowing public discussion. They contribute well when talking
about the city budget but less effectively when discussing such
nonquantifiable subjects as community values. Assign them the
role of recorder or secretary and they will be so conscientious
about watching over the accuracy of what everyone else says
that they will not have time to split hairs themselves.

Jump-Ups. Excitable, enthusiastic, high-energy cheerlead-
ers who are more interested in style than substance and have
no patience with deliberate thinkers, jump-ups can be catalysts
for getting a slow group going. They may also engender hostility, however, especially if they interrupt too often (as if their
ideas were the only ones worth noting). Do not call on jump-
ups for their opinions; you will hear from them soon enough.
Turn to others for substantive discussion. Do not make them
recorders or summarizers, either, because their handwriting is
often as nervous-looking as they are; furthermore, they may
write down only their own ideas.

Know-It-Alls. "I've lived in this town since before many
of you were born, and let me tell you, those new ideas will
never work." Or, "I'm a registered engineer, and I know that
you can't build a sewer system that way." By the law of aver-
ages, know-it-alls are right some of the time, and sometimes
they are half-right. Most often, however, they are noisy inter-
rupters who will disrupt the group process if you let them. Acknowledge their expertise only if it applies specifically to this
situation. "Yes, it's really helpful to have an engineer with your
knowledge of sewers, but even those of us without a technical
background need to have a say about how we want to pay for
them." If their credentials do not apply, say so: "I understand
that your field is electronics. I'm not sure how that relates to
sewers. The civil engineers who've studied this project tell us

it's feasible." If know-it-alls continue their rude behavior, encourage the group (which does not like them any more than you do) to take discipline in their own hands, and they will. "I'm sure you'll admit, Bernie, that we're all as qualified as you are to make this decision."

Laggards. Whereas dropouts generally find a seat quietly in back, laggards amble in late and move to the front — visibly and often audibly — stepping over and around anyone in their way. Their haughty manner indicates that they think the meeting should begin when they arrive. They try to interrupt the proceedings by asking a question to enable them to catch up: "I know you may have covered this already, but . . . ." As the leader confronted with chronic laggards, do not show your displeasure with a scowl. They will not notice, and the rest of the group may be offended. Still, you need not put up with persistent interruptions. Offer to meet them at the break or after the meeting to fill them in. "We have a tight agenda, and I know the rest of you want to move right along." If you always start on time, laggards will realize that when you are in charge, they miss important parts of the meeting by being chronically late.

Sneak-Outers. People who come on time but rudely disrupt the continuity or momentum of a meeting by leaving abruptly, usually without an explanation, may really have an emergency. Most times, however, they are registering a nonverbal protest against the subject, the format, or the organizers of the meeting. (Some, of course, just lack manners.) Whatever their motives, the group leader must not legitimize their behavior. Spying a sneak-outer, one inexperienced moderator interrupted her presentation with an inept attempt at humor: "Oh no, Mary's leaving. She's really going to miss something. We should have locked the door." She thus called attention to behavior that half the group had not noticed — and the sneak-outer sneaked out anyway. Discourage sneaking out by suggesting a verbal contract with the participants at the beginning of the meeting: "According to our agenda, we're going to have a two-hour meeting. Is there anyone who has to leave early?" Deprived of their primary weapon — the element of surprise — sneak-outers just might stay put.

Stand-Patters. Do not waste your time trying to confuse some people with the facts; they have their own stubborn opinions and will not budge. Stand-patters are rarely interested in anyone else's point of view; even documentary evidence will not convince them. "So what if those radicals say that the river is polluted. When I was a kid we never had a fancy pool at the high school. If the old swimming hole was good enough for us, it should be good enough today." Sometimes stand-patters' obstinacy can have a positive effect by causing the other group members to think through their opinions and defend them with facts and figures. As the leader, you must give stand-patters time to state their case, but when it becomes obvious that their opinions are not shared by the others, move on.

Single-Issuers. Whatever the stated agenda, some people come to all meetings with the same point of view. If group members know these single-issuers from past experience, they will smile indulgently while listening to their spiel and then go on about the real business of the meeting. Even if no one has seen them before, they give themselves away soon enough by their persistent narrow-mindedness and disinterest in topics other than their own. These people are usually harmless and just want to be heard. Let the single-issuers speak — once — but do not respond if they are way off target. Quickly direct your attention to getting the meeting back on the agenda. Sometimes the only way to keep single-issuers out of mischief is to appoint them to a subcommittee — of one. "Jason, no one else seems to be interested in the life cycle of the beetle, so why don't you look it up and get back to us?" With any luck, he will miss your next meeting because of another, where he is more assured of a sympathetic audience.

Talkers. Many meetings are attended by someone who pontificates too much, too loudly, and too long. Like stand-patters, they are opinionated, but they have an added obnoxious characteristic: an overbearing attitude. Though they blurt out opinions without discretion, they expect to be taken seriously on everything they say. If a talker has status with the group — is the president of the organization, or the mayor, for example — you may have to put up with the speeches during discussion. But at the first break, take the talker aside and ask, "Am I in error in thinking that the goal of the meeting is to get other people's opinions?" The talker should understand your message and quiet down. If the talker is not a VIP, overcome your natural tendency to move away and actually move closer. This is especially effective if the talker is seated. Stand up close, wait for the talker to take a breath, and say, politely but firmly, "Thank you" — nothing more. Then redirect the discussion to the subject at hand and turn to the others in the group. Summarize what the talker said only if it is relevant to the discussion.

Walkers. Sometimes people pace at length. If these walkers leave the meeting at an inappropriate time, they become walkers. Like sneak-outers, they want to call attention to themselves, but they do so with a flourish. Stomping from the scene, they may exclaim, "I can't stand any more of this." The silent treatment is best. Walkers lose status and credibility as soon as they run away.

Groupies. The behavior of groups as well as individuals can present a challenge to leaders of a meeting. People who come to the meeting as a clique often make sure that they are noticed by waving placards or posters, yelling and shouting, marching and demonstrating. They hope that by showing strength and cohesiveness, they can intimidate the sponsors and disrupt the proceedings. They are often more interested in calling attention to their cause, especially if the media are present, than in influencing others to join them or even in affecting the outcome of the proceedings.

In the heat of battle, it may seem that they speak for the majority, but despite their organized ferocity, they are usually a minority and should be treated as such.

> *More than 100 people came to a community meeting to talk about alternative ways to finance the public school system. They picked up their numbered name tags and information packets and gathered around the refreshment table. The organizers were surprised and delighted at the large turnout and looked forward to a spirited discussion. Just before the meeting began, a group of people entered, obviously together.*

Carrying handmade placards declaring, "No new taxes,"
they started to organize a demonstration.
    The five-foot-two chair walked over to the six-foot-
two leader. "Thank you for coming, sir; I hope that you
and your friends will all go to your numbered tables. We're
just about ready to begin, and we only have two hours to
cover a lot of ground." Expecting to be treated rudely, he
was taken aback by her politeness. "Well," he sputtered,
"we don't want a sales tax rammed down our throats, and
we want to make sure that everyone knows it." "I under-
stand," she answered. "Why don't you put your signs up
against the wall? That way everyone can see them, but you'll
be able to participate in the meeting." He reluctantly told
his followers to lower their signs and play by the rules.
"Okay, I can see that you really mean business," he said.
The chairperson's cordial but no-nonsense approach defused
a potentially unpleasant scene and won plaudits from the
majority of the more reasonable members of the audience.

When dealing with groups of people, just as with individuals, it is important to remain even-tempered. When they
shout, be reasonable. When they talk rapidly, speak slowly and
deliberately. If there is time, the chair may give them five
minutes or so to state their views. But in giving, the chair re-
tains the authority to take away, and that prerogative must be
made clear.

    If a group disruption occurs during the presentation part
of the meeting and the audience becomes noticeably restless,
call a short break and then move on to the discussion phase.
In that way, you remove any chance for them to take over the
meeting. Remember that the majority in the audience is reasonable and will back you if you are fair and remain in control.

The very nature of a public meeting — a place where human beings interact and controversial issues are discussed — is fertile
territory for all manner of people with distinct personalities and
points of view. The alert leader acts to minimize or neutralize
the problems, knowing that the majority will be grateful for such
decisiveness.

8

Positive Media Relations

Many managers and executives are convinced that anyone connected with the media is a pest, a nemesis, an adversary — at best, a necessary evil. In their opinion, the media intrude upon their private lives and public agendas by asking unwarranted and unwanted questions, distorting the truth, following their own agendas, and generally impeding relationships between their agency and the public.

On the other hand, the media see themselves as guardians of the people's right to know and the conveyers of truth and information that otherwise would be hidden or at least obscured by public agencies having little or no regard for the public good.

There are abundant examples supporting both points of view, though the truth most often lies somewhere in between. But the facts of present-day public life cannot be denied: the media are here to stay, and managers and others who plan and direct public meetings ignore them at their peril. Moreover, whatever their faults, the media are not part of a monolithic conspiracy plotting to trap the unwary. They are separate and extremely competitive businesses whose practitioners take their jobs seriously.

To deal with the media effectively, it is important, first, to recognize their distinct characteristics. Just as there is an obvious physical difference between print and television and between the latter and radio, so are there distinct differences in their modes of operation.

Next, accept the fact that media representatives are generalists; you are the specialist. In most cases, you and your staff know more than they on the subjects that you want them to cover. It is your responsibility, therefore, to distill your information into a form that they can understand and then convey to the public. Make sure that your media releases are clear and comprehensive, and you are more likely to receive the attention that you think you deserve. In one short paragraph, present the essence of your message. If you are announcing a meeting, describe what will happen if the report/recommendation/project that is the subject of the meeting is accepted. What will happen if it is not? What will be the effect on the schools, seniors, local economy, quality of life, or any other factors of importance?

Successful relations with the media are never one-way, and those executives who try to "manage" the news rarely succeed for long.

The nervous secretary interrupts the harried city manager's staff meeting to say that a local television reporter is on the phone. He takes the call and the reporter says, "We understand that you've found a major ring of thieves inside city hall — thieves who have stolen thousands of dollars of valuable equipment in the last eight months. I'll be right over with a camera to find out what you intend to do about it." The city manager is noticeably upset. He stutters as he objects, "Well, we weren't going to release that to the public until tomorrow night, when we have our regular city council meeting. We still have some loose ends to tie up." The reporter is persistent, citing the public's right to know — now. The city manager reluctantly agrees to see the reporter in fifteen minutes, leaving himself barely enough time to gulp down a cup of coffee with two aspirin.

The interview does not go well; the reporter implies that there is a cover-up, and the city manager feels trapped,

saying much more than he should. That evening he is dis-
mayed to hear the local television news anchor — who, by
the way, was not the person who interviewed him — begin
the program with, "In an exclusive interview today, the city
manager reluctantly revealed to our news staff that there is
a major theft scandal at city hall. Is this a cover-up? Well,
you judge for yourselves."

When faced with forceful, pushy media representatives, even individuals accustomed to making decisions and being in charge let the media control them. In this case, the city manager — surprised and dismayed that news of the alleged theft had leaked out before the public meeting — still did not have to grant the media interview immediately. He could have said, "I'm sorry, but I have an urgent appointment now. I'll be glad to see you in two hours." Delay for good reasons is acceptable. Stonewalling — "I can't give you any information," "No comment" — is not. It raises a red flag to the media and gives the impression that you have something to hide. The city manager had every right to give himself a little time to collect his thoughts, review pertinent material, and ask principals in the investigation to join him in the interview — in other words, to control as many factors as possible.

Even if the intrusive reporter and camera person had appeared on the city manager's doorstep, he could have asked them to wait at least as long as it took to catch his breath and get the staff he needed to back him up. Then he could have held the keys to a successful media interview: controlling as many factors as possible and maintaining poise when matters threaten to get out of hand.

Before any media encounter — whether on the phone, on the scene, or in the studio — ask reporters what they want to talk about. This gives you a chance to decide generally what you will say and how you will say it. If you are interviewed over the phone and are particularly apprehensive that you may get rattled and not say exactly what you want to, jot down an outline. Notes will help you stay on track, and no one but yourself can see them. If you have successfully stalled for time, fulfill your end of the bargain by returning the phone call or being available for the personal interview when you promised.

An effective manager is willing to share the glory as well as the blame — and certainly the responsibility — whenever possible. To reinforce your reliability and responsiveness, bring in everyone else involved: elected officials, staff people, consultants on whose reports you are relying. Get together beforehand and rehearse, to make sure that you know what each of you will say. Try for a consistent, clear message.

Whenever possible, hold the interview in your office, on other familiar turf, or on a site of your choice that illustrates the issue well. In other words, control the territory. A television studio is the least friendly and most intimidating setting. As discussed in the section about television, these negative factors can be overcome; but whenever possible, be proactive. If, for example, you are talking to reporters about open public forums to discuss the state's fiscal crisis, your message will be most effectively conveyed if you are photographed in your office, at your desk. You want to be surrounded by trappings that send the message that this public servant is working diligently on a serious problem. On the other hand, if you are being interviewed about neighborhood meetings to discuss your community's new mandatory recycling program, go to the town dump and suggest the mass of solid waste as the backdrop. By creating such photographic opportunities, you are likely to receive better television and newspaper coverage than if you held the same interview in your office.

Learn a lesson from astute politicians: never fall for baited or leading questions. The city manager in the earlier property theft example could have blunted the reporter's sensationalist tone by putting the matter into perspective: "Yes, we certainly are concerned when anything is stolen from the city. But I think it's important to note that the value of the typewriters and calculators we lost is about three thousand dollars, while we have two million dollars worth of office equipment safe and sound." Or he could have challenged the reporter's assumption of a conspiracy: "That's not my information. Where did you get the idea that hundreds of items have been stolen?"

Professional and technical people are often misquoted, because they are not accustomed to speaking in headlines or "sound bites." Be quotable by avoiding long and complicated sentences. Distill your message into five or ten words, in simple English, and you will be pleasantly surprised at how often you are quoted directly and completely.

On the other hand, do not be reluctant to say those three little words, "I don't know," as long as you add, "I'll get the information for you." Do not pretend to be the expert on everything, but volunteer to help the reporter find out or assign a staff person to get on it immediately. There may be times when you cannot tell everything you know, but you should never tell an untruth.

Never say anything that you do not want to see repeated. Even if you insist that something is off the record, reporters — while honoring your confidence — may validate what you have said with others and then repeat the substance without attributing it to you.

A good way to help ensure that the media understand your point of view is to summarize at the end of the interview, reiterating the points that you have made and asking reporters if they have any additional issues to discuss or clarify. Still, you can never completely control how a story is reported, and you should not try to. Never ask to review the reporter's story before it is printed, for example. You will certainly be rebuffed and perhaps resented for wanting this unwarranted control.

Reaching Out

There are many ways to be proactive in obtaining the attention of the media, and through them, the public.

An effective approach, though one not often used by public agencies because it takes time, is to stage an event. As was noted previously, the media are more likely to attend an interview or announcement if you hold it at an interesting and photogenic location; likewise, the public interest is aroused more readily when you go "on location." Try to share the spotlight with sure-fire subjects, such as children or old people. If you are holding a public forum on children's safety, for example, announce it on a playground or near a particularly dangerous school crossing. Ask concerned parents, teachers, and children to back you up, and be sure that they get in any picture. Or sponsor an essay contest on the subject and announce the winners at their schools, all the while calling attention to the scheduled public meetings on the subject. Announcing a public meeting to discuss regulating nursing homes? Invite the media to an appropriate facility— preferably one that meets your criteria rather than a bad example, unless you really want to stir up controversy.

Public service announcements (PSAs) are useful, but they require work. In the not-too-distant past, radio and television stations were required to provide a certain amount of time in the public interest in order to keep their Federal Communications Commission licenses. This is no longer the case, and many stations are reluctant to give away precious air time. It is now necessary to court most station managers and news and public service directors and convince them that public-spiritedly promoting your event will be of value to them and their ratings.

If your cause captures their attention, some will cover the entire cost—and it can be thousands of dollars—to develop a fifteen- or thirty-second public service announcement; others will air an announcement free if it is produced elsewhere. Explore the possibilities with your local radio and TV managers. Well-written and -produced PSAs are very effective ways to announce public meetings to the general community.

Surveys of newspaper readers have shown that the letters to the editor are second in popularity only to sports. Guest editorials are also widely read. Letters that are brief and state a thoughtful point of view are most likely to be published. That point of view is more credible if it is expressed by a layperson rather than a governmental official. For example, "As chair of the citizens' budget committee, I urge everyone to be involved in the important fiscal decisions that our town has to make." Offer to ghostwrite a letter or article for a sympathetic citizens' committee or advisory board or to review the facts if they want to write it themselves. Call the paper's editor for rules about length, style, deadlines, and similar matters.

The media release is a common, inexpensive, much-used form of communication between public agencies and the media. It can be effective if used in combination with other methods, but it should not be relied upon entirely to entice the media to cover your event. Too many releases get trashed because they are addressed to the wrong person, are received too late, are not written succinctly and clearly, or do not portray the sense of importance or urgency the issue deserves.

The newly appointed associate director of the local housing agency complained that the agency had not received press coverage for its last few events. "I don't know what to do to get their attention," she complained. "I purposely send out media releases in an unmarked envelope. People are so suspicious of government nowadays that I don't want the editor to prejudge us." It is too bad that she wastes her time with such misplaced modesty. The editor or secretary probably throws the envelopes away without opening them just because they are unmarked! Not only should you always use official stationery, but whenever possible enclose a personal note from the director, the mayor, or another suitable VIP. This will reinforce the importance of the message and help you obtain the attention that your agency deserves.

How up-to-date is your mailing list of media contacts? Media professionals are especially peripatetic. People move out, on, or up just when they learn the old job. Update your list at least every six months. If you do not have a list, start one. Have a staff person call all your local media—press, radio, and television, including cable—and ask for the names of the people to whom you should address information about your agency. If in doubt about the appropriate recipient, send your release to the editor in chief or city editor of newspapers and the manager or assignment editor of radio and TV stations.

Take special care to spell the name of your recipient correctly. Even if the editor tells you over the phone that his name is John Smith—how straightforward can you get?—ask him how to spell it. He could be a Jon Smythe. Lori or Laurie, Sandi or Sandy, male or female—you get the idea: never take anyone's name for granted.

Always indicate a release date. "For immediate release" is the most common and means that the information can be used when it is received. If needed, be more specific: "For release after 2 P.M. June 5."

Write in the traditional who, what, when, where, and how format still honored by the journalistic profession, but preface your narrative with a headline to get your readers' attention. "Accident at School Crossing Spurs Community Meeting" is more likely to interest the media and the public than the accurate but more mundane "Agency Holds Community Meeting About Safety."

In a brief introductory paragraph, give the bare facts of your meeting. Additional pertinent information (and eye-catching quotes) can be included in subsequent paragraphs. Never write more than one page (double-spaced), although you can include attachments. Conclude with the traditional journalistic ending (-30-) to show that you know what you're doing. (See Exhibit 8.1.)

Exhibit 8.1. Sample Media Release (should be double-spaced).

City-County Housing Authority
222 Elm Street
Hometown, OR 12345

FOR IMMEDIATE RELEASE
Contact Alice Brown, Assistant Director, 555-1234

Tenant Pet-Denial Policy Subject of Public Meeting

The city-county housing authority will hold a public meeting Wednesday, July 10, at 7 P.M. to evaluate its policy that denies tenants the right to have any pets besides birds and goldfish. The meeting will be held in the agency's auditorium, 222 Elm Street.

The agency is reconsidering its policy after hearing from elderly residents that they would feel less lonely and more secure if they had a dog or a cat as a pet. Other residents say that their small apartments will not accommodate large pets and want a size and weight limit. People with all points of view will be encouraged to speak at the meeting.

"We are open to any suggestions that will increase the feeling of safety and comfort of our clients without inconveniencing others," said Brenden Block, agency director.

-30-

A media advisory is a good way to pique the media's interest enough to call you and perhaps even to provide live coverage. Send a short release four or five days before the event, indicating that more information will be available at the meeting. The facsimile machine enables you to send your release without having to rely on the sometimes unpredictable postal service, but you still need to give the media the proper lead time. Always call a day before to remind the people to whom you have written—and do not be dismayed if they say (as most will) that they cannot remember receiving your notice or that they have misplaced it. That is when the fax machine is really handy; you can obligingly send them another immediately. When you speak to them personally, or even if you have to leave a message, apprise them of any special story, photo, or interview opportunity that may be of particular interest to their public. (See Exhibit 8.2.)

Exhibit 8.2. Sample Press Advisory.

Tenant Pet-Denial Policy Subject of Public Meeting

The City-County Housing Authority will hold a public meeting Wednesday, July 10, at 7 p.m. to evaluate its policy that denies tenants the right to have any pets besides birds and goldfish. The meeting will be held in the agency's auditorium, 222 Elm Street.

-30-

Getting the Media to Announce Your Meeting

Although there are generalities that apply to dealing with all the media, each facet of this industry is distinct.

Print

With tape recordings now commonplace, the electronic media have more permanence than previously. Still, TV and radio are generally more transitory than written articles, which may be read at leisure or clipped for further reference. Yet even in print—the most permanent of the media—experienced journalists are humbled at least once in their careers by seeing an especially thoughtful piece lining a birdcage or garbage can.

Do not limit your attempts at print coverage to the local newspaper. In most communities, there are college, high school, and neighborhood papers; church, community, and organizational newsletters; special-interest magazines; and throwaway shoppers—all read by different segments of the public. If you focus on the aspects of your story that are most likely to interest a narrow niche of readers, you will find that smaller presses will give you more space than general circulation newspapers, which have to reach many more competing interests.

Consider, for example, the general media release in Exhibit 8.1, announcing a public meeting to reconsider the pet-ownership policy of the local public housing agency. In addition to the general-purpose newspaper, the print media likely to give this coverage are the senior citizens' newspaper, the local veterinary association newsletter, and the neighborhood shopper. The general information—date, time, place—is the same for all. But the angle, or what in the trade is called the "news peg," varies to suit the audience.

For the senior citizens' newspaper, emphasize that the agency is considering the change in policy in response to requests by some of its elderly residents. Enclose a photo of one or two gray-haired tenant leaders conferring with the agency director, or suggest where such a photo might be taken. Include quotes from tenants favorable to the openness of the agency in considering their request.

Another approach is necessary to interest the veterinarians in publicizing the meeting. Not unsympathetic to oldsters, they are more interested in how this issue will have an impact on their professional practices and the possibility of obtaining more clients. They might be flattered to be invited to the public meeting as outside experts—an invitation that would also give credence to the agency's claim that it wants to do the right thing.

The news release to the veterinarians' organization should stress the types of animals being considered and note that if the policy is modified, it will be important to make sure that seniors know how to care for their pets. The veterinarians might also be interested in volunteering their services for a monthly pet-care clinic or providing ongoing care for residents' pets at reduced fees.

The housing agency also wants to reach the general citizen, of course. The local all-purpose newspaper will probably give the meeting one paragraph buried on the back page, but the shopper, distributed free to every household, is inclined to be more generous with coverage of community events.

The angle that interests the shopper's editor may be neighborhood safety, or perhaps the pros and cons of reconsidering a policy that gives low-income tenants the same privileges as citizens who live elsewhere. Your release might stress that comments from the entire community are welcome, as evidence that the housing agency realizes its obligation to all citizens. Photos are nearly always welcome, especially if you provide a glossy print. Combine children with seniors and you have a sure winner.

Columnists are another outlet for your story. Every community has at least one who is read and quoted widely. Read the columns over time to get a sense of their style and general content. Most columnists write about human interest—the news behind the news.

In our pet-policy example, the veterinarians' donation of time, particularly if one vet is a leading citizen of the community, might be the angle that the local columnist would use. Your release could focus on that, but make sure that the housing agency's public meeting receives appropriate notice too.

Be alert to feature opportunities in other parts of the general-purpose newspaper—for example, letters to the editor and opinion articles (discussed earlier). Perhaps there is even the possibility of editorial support. Know your local editor and others who shape the editorial policy of the newspaper well enough that you can call them if there is a crisis and they can call you if they want inside information. The two-way nurturing of open communication and trust will pay off when you need it. You may not always get the editorial approval you want, but you are more likely to be treated fairly and with respect.

The key to dealing successfully with the print media is to realize their variety and segmentation and assign someone to spend the time ferreting out the angles that will get you the greatest coverage with the audience you want most to reach.

If all else fails to garner the publicity you want, pay for it! The decision to do so is not made easily by most public agencies with budget restrictions, but neither should it be discarded out of hand. The advantages are twofold: you can choose the medium and you can completely control the message.

> *A council of governments in a growing urban area recently embarked on an ambitious program of sponsoring community meetings about the pressing issues of growth and transportation. After failing to interest either of the two daily newspapers in printing articles of any size or depth, the agency produced and paid for its own twelve-page, four-color supplement, which was inserted in the Sunday papers. They reached 750,000 people, and the council saw the fruits of its labors and expenditures rewarded. This single, ambitious, expensive effort increased interest and attendance at the public meetings. As a by-product, the project finally attracted free media attention; reporters realized that these issues did concern a broad range of citizens.*

Television

One of the most important differences between print and the electronic media — television and radio — is the amount of coverage that you can expect. As noted previously, there are many possibilities for stories of some length and depth in the various print media. Generally, however, the most television news coverage to which a public agency can aspire is the few words that fill up fifteen or thirty seconds. Professionals who want to get their points across on TV need to master the political technique of the sound bite or headline.

Most public administrators are understandably intimidated by the brash and inquisitorial reporter who pushes a microphone in their face, but there are ways to take control of even that formidable situation.

If reporters corner you at a controversial public meeting, keep cool. Ask them to turn off the camera and mike and give you some idea of the issues that they want to cover. Then request a few minutes to comb your hair, go to the bathroom, and ask a staff person or another public official to join you. In other words, take whatever time you can to collect your thoughts.

Answer questions in a short, succinct, headline style. Taking advantage of whatever time you have, speak in brief, snappy phrases (ten words or fewer) that convey your basic message. Your ability to communicate succinctly and clearly will pay off when you see your ten-minute interview reduced to a ten-second news headline without distortion.

Remembering that television is a visual medium, dress the part whenever you expect or suspect an interview. Your credibility is conveyed by the nonverbal message of how you look before you say anything. When deciding what to wear, consider your audience: what do they expect the regional forest director, state welfare manager, or local public works supervisor to look like? In the office, you may work comfortably in your shirtsleeves or a simple blouse and skirt; but for a television interview, put on a jacket. Your attire must convey an impression of professionalism and competence, and the camera will most likely focus on you from the waist up.

On television, less is more. Wear solid colors in contrasting combinations — dark suit and white or pastel shirt, small-patterned tie for men; suit or dress with simple lines for women. Steer clear of stripes and plaids, loud ties, deep, revealing necklines, and clinky or shiny rings, bracelets, earrings, and cufflinks.

If you are using graphs or charts to explain your point, prepare an extra set, reduced in size, to give the interviewer. It is a good idea to write a short summary of detailed technical information as well, but do not be disappointed if neither is used by the reporter.

Look directly at the camera, not at the interviewer. Think of the camera as representing the vast viewing public, and look directly into it — not at the interviewer. You want to appear to be speaking directly to them.

For most administrators, an interview in the television studio is the most difficult media situation. You can exercise a modicum of control when interviewed in your own office, on the site, or even at the public meeting you organized; but under the glaring lights and artificial, show-business atmosphere of the TV studio, you may feel totally out of control. All the principles of TV interviewing that we have discussed previously — particularly attention to dress and the ability to speak succinctly — are important in helping you be successful in the studio, but there are others to consider.

The week or day before your interview, watch the program on which you will be interviewed. Familiarize yourself with the format and the set, the style and technique of the hosts. Are they friendly and generally informed? Inquisitorial and probing? Gabby and controlling? Laid-back, letting their guests do most of the talking? Do they seem to have a bias or a particular point of view? What time of day is the program aired? Retired people and women are most likely to watch morning and afternoon TV, while the age and gender of the audience are more varied in the evening. How long is your segment of the program, and what role are you expected to play? Advocate? Resource? Defender of a controversial action or project? Are you being interviewed solo or as part of a panel? Knowing the background before you appear at the studio helps you prepare to give the appropriate responses.

Both men and women look better on TV with the addition of some theatrical cover-up. A hint of blusher adds a healthy glow; facial powder covers perspiring brows and shiny heads, foreheads, and noses. Find out if the studio provides makeup services, and if so, accept them gratefully. If not, whatever your gender, bring along the proper makeup and retire to the restroom beforehand for a touch-up.

At least an hour before, limit your beverage intake to water. Avoid alcohol and caffeine of all kinds, including colas, coffee, and tea. They all have a drying effect on what is probably an already tight-with-anticipation throat.

Once the interview begins, ignore the people running around the set with headphones plastered to their ears. They are taking their cues from the director, who is in the sound booth, far removed from the action on the floor.

When you are speaking, do not try to catch a glimpse of yourself on the nearby monitor. Likewise, avoid trying to figure out which one of the several cameras is focusing on you. The director is making split-second decisions about cameras and all other aspects of the show, so concentrate on your job, which is to look and sound your best.

Pretend that you are in the second grade again and will get marked down for fidgeting, smirking, or looking bored or disgusted—especially when another person is speaking. These spontaneous reactions may be just the ones that the director and camera pick up, to your later dismay.

Understand the importance of body language in reinforcing your image as a credible, trustworthy person. Lean forward to appear friendly and relaxed; sit up straight to emphasize a serious point. Do not smirk, frown, slump, or drape your arm casually over your neighbor's chair. To defuse a hostile or difficult question, smile. Give the viewing audience the impression that you can be trusted. Do not look furtively around the room or stare at the floor or ceiling; people associate such behavior with deceptiveness.

If you know that you will be seated on the set, will it be behind or around a table or on low couches or chairs? Practice sitting in various positions in front of a mirror at home until you find one that is comfortable and looks good; women should wear a skirt or dress that covers their knees. Keep your feet on the floor and your hands in your lap. This grounding helps you keep control.

If your purpose is to advertise an upcoming public meeting and the host is veering off the subject, be alert for opportunities to get back on track: "I'm glad you brought that up. That's one reason we're eager to hear what the public has to say at our meeting next week." If confronted with an unfair personal attack, state your perspective or position in an affirmative, nondefensive, firm, and honest manner: "I can see where some people would see it that way, but the truth is . . . ."

Do not be intimidated by the "pregnant pause"—the reporter's way of goading you into filling a silence and saying something unexpected. After you have answered a question, maintain eye contact, smile, take a drink of water, even blink, but do not say any more than you intended.

Avoid jargon or technical words that your host and the audience will not understand. Practice the message that you want to convey until it is simple and clear.

When it is all over, watch a tape recording of the program in the comfort of your own living room, alone or with a trusted friend or relative. Be critical. Do you look and sound credible? Is your message clear and succinct? Have you avoided jargon and concepts that are difficult to understand? Are you convincing? Would you be motivated to come to your event or meeting? If you fall short in any area, take this as a cue to improve for your next television opportunity.

Radio

Of the three primary media, radio is the most intimate. It is most often background, rather than primary, to your audience of one—rarely more—who is listening while doing something else in the car, bathroom, office, kitchen, or workshop. To capture the listener's attention, you must train yourself to speak in fragments or ten-word headlines so that whenever listeners tune in, they should be able to get some type of positive message. While the same general rules about the media apply also to radio, there are some special things to consider.

First, there are probably more radio than TV stations in your community. This gives radio a distinct advantage if you want to reach specific segments of the public. Assign a staff person to find out the focus of each station—news, music (what kind?), talk, national, local, or some mixture—by calling the program manager or a friendly advertising firm that places ads in specific markets. A news or music station with no live segments or interviews might still be induced to read a notice of your public meeting if you send a media release. Know the demographics of each station's listeners and key your release to each. If, for example, the station plays "oldies" for the fifty-years-and-older set, be sure to mention those meeting sites that are particularly accessible to the handicapped and/or the elderly.

An all-talk radio station, on the other hand, is hungry for guests — especially articulate local people — and would probably welcome your willingness to talk with the host and listening audience about your agency's upcoming community meetings.

Welcome opportunities to be interviewed on talk shows as a way to reach a different segment of the public. As for a television appearance, prepare by listening to the radio program beforehand so that you know the format, the host's general attitude, and the types of questions that may be asked. One important advantage of radio over TV is that the audience cannot see you. You can wear your most comfortable clothes, slump, drape your arm over a chair — even grimace and frown, as long as facial expressions do not affect the quality of your voice, which should be warm and friendly. Answer questions in the same friendly, nondefensive way we discussed previously.

Some radio stations will air public service announcements — and even help you record them, if you write the script — even though they are no longer required to do so by the federal government. Develop a friendly relationship with the program manager and you will have a better chance of having your announcement aired during prime listening time rather than at 3 A.M.

If you decide to buy advertising, radio is the least expensive of the mass media.

When the Media Come to Your Meeting

All the tips that have been provided so far are for one general purpose: to help your agency reach the public through the media and interest them in attending your meeting or event. Well, suppose you are successful; the media *are* interested. They air your announcement, interview you or others, and generally spread the word. The public comes, but so do the media. Now what do you do?

It is very important that one staff person be given responsibility for the care and feeding of the media before, during, and after the meeting — preferably the person who was the principal media contact before the event. At the meeting itself, that job starts with finding and greeting media representatives as they come in the door. Only the TV camera people are obvious; reporters and others look like ordinary folk, especially if they are not carrying note pads. Ask everyone to sign in with name, affiliation, and phone number, and then scan the list for media people you may have missed.

Whenever possible, prepare and hand out a media kit. It should include the release that you sent them (which they may not have read), the agenda of the meeting, and background information that will help them report accurately on the event. Offer to introduce them to VIPs from the agency or elsewhere, and be otherwise helpful and accommodating. Most media people guard their hard-boiled personas carefully, and though they rarely say thanks for these courtesies, they nevertheless appreciate and remember them and may reward you with accurate and full coverage.

Decide in advance where to set up those bulky and intrusive TV cameras. If left to themselves, camera people will choose a spot right in front—the place most convenient for them but distracting to the audience and the presenters. Find a place for the camera that is as unobtrusive as possible but that still allows for the best camera angles. Remove any audience chairs right behind the cameras before people have claimed them. Television lights are not as blinding as they used to be, and cameras are more quiet. They are tolerated in most courtrooms today, and with the goodwill and cooperation of all parties can be accommodated at your public meeting.

After the meeting, contact each of the media that you notified but that did not show up and give them an oral or written summary of the results of the meeting.

When the Media Err

You have done everything to ensure that the media have the right information and are motivated to come to your meeting, and you think that you have given them sufficient tender, loving care to ensure positive results. All they need to do is report the story accurately. How dismaying, then, to hear the evening

TV news anchor get it all wrong: "With much reluctance, tonight our city housing agency agreed to let residents have pets, as long as they don't bark or mess on their neighbors' grass. One violation and the pet will be taken away." Another reporter then interviews an elderly resident whom you have never seen before. The resident holds up a little poodle and says, "It's been a long time since I diapered a kid, but the housing people say I have to resort to that with my new puppy." The next day's newspaper headline reads, "Pet Owners Storm Meeting to Demand Their Rights." The article, hardly more fair than the TV coverage the night before, quotes concerned residents who commented before the meeting even began, burying in the fourth paragraph information that the meeting was amicable, that the vote to allow pets was unanimous, and that no one really "stormed" at or in anything.

If you have followed all the advice in this chapter, such inaccurate reporting is likely to be an infrequent occurrence. Still, if it does happen, you and your staff will be understandably angry and upset. There are several steps you can take, but never consider any of them until after you and everyone else concerned with the issue have had a chance to get the reactions of others more dispassionate. You may find that you are supersensitive, that most people did not notice what you consider grievous errors. If you still believe that you were injured, you can take several steps.

First, analyze the offending reporting objectively. Is it really inaccurate, or is it just another way of stating information? Leaving the question of libel and defamation to the attorneys, you should be concerned with how facts are stated. If you find that the headline is offensive but the story is relatively accurate, do not take any action. Newspaper headline writers are chosen for their speed, not accuracy. They are often ensconced in a cloistered part of the office and sheltered from the facts as much as possible; facing impossible deadlines, they attempt to fit a few descriptive words into a certain space. Editors of neighborhood or community newspapers are responsible for their own headlines, but they too are harried, beset with many responsibilities. Headline writers are allowed to take license with the truth to fit the newspaper's layout requirements, and in most cases the public agency has very little leverage to complain — especially if that is the only problem.

The same can be said about the television coverage. In our example, agency representatives did express concern about protecting neighbors against unruly animals, but this was during the introductory part of the meeting. Unfortunately, the TV camera person and reporter left to meet a deadline and were neither briefed by a staff representative about what else was likely to occur nor called later by the agency with information about what they missed. They had no way of knowing, therefore, that the agency would agree to a public information campaign about responsible pet ownership instead of the fines and removal of offending animals that were first considered. The TV coverage was not in error; it just reported only part of the story. The station would probably welcome a call from the agency to update the story. This follow-up is likely to result in additional, positive coverage.

What about the newspaper, radio, or TV editorial that disagrees with your position and proclaims, "The housing agency made a stupid decision last night to allow its tenants to own pets. Low-income people have little enough resources as it is. Now some of them will probably starve themselves for their worthless animals." The editor or station manager based that opinion on fact; he or she just reached a different conclusion than you would have preferred. It is fruitless to take exception to the media's right to state an opinion. In considering rebuttal, you might suggest that your constituents (not staff) start a letter-writing campaign. You might also try to have your reasons for approving pets given equal time in a guest editorial.

In assessing the extent of wrongdoing, examine all the facts. Was the treatment of the story untrue? Half-true? Or are you just unhappy with the emphasis? Were names or titles misspelled or were comments mistakenly attributed? Does the story damage your reputation or that of the agency or unfairly represent the situation? If you think that you have a legitimate complaint, start your complaining low in the organization. If you know the reporter, call her first: "Phyllis, we really appreciate your covering our meeting on pets yesterday, especially on such a hot night. But I think that you left before we decided on our public information campaign on responsible pet ownership. I'll be glad to get you in touch with the veterinarians who are heading up the program." You have gently chided the reporter but also given her another story—a win/win situation that should always be your goal. Another approach: "Helen, thanks for the coverage of last night's meeting. But your headline writer seems to have gotten the wrong impression about the attitudes of our tenants." Resist yelling, "Where did your lamebrained headline writer get the idea that people were storming the meeting?" Although you are uncomfortable with the headline, be savvy enough not to hold the reporter responsible. You then can add, "I'd be glad to arrange follow-up interviews with some of our tenants who think that this is the greatest thing since sliced bread." Another win/win.

If you do not know the reporter well, or if you have good reason from prior dealings to distrust her, contact the next-highest person responsible: the editor of that particular department, of the whole newspaper, or the program or station manager. Be sure of your facts, and do not rant and rave. People in these positions deal with angry readers/viewers all the time, and they are likely to dismiss you as just another crank unless you present your case reasonably and ask for a retraction or a correction.

Newspapers usually have a space set aside for corrections. If the people you contact disagree with you or refuse to present a correct version, ask the editor if he will accept a letter to the editor or a signed opinion column. It is more difficult to convince TV and radio stations to correct mistakes, though some electronic media do give air time for citizens to express their differences.

In those few cases of absolute misrepresentation, you may want to ask the governor or the highest political official in your jurisdiction to intervene, but this is a tactic used only sparingly.

Yes, the media, which comprise human beings, do make mistakes: by omission, commission, and sometimes—but more seldom than you may think—by plain meanness and malice.

But do not allow yourself to get upset easily. Choose your battle-field carefully. Work toward a positive, mutual interdependence — you on them to convey the news, and they on you as a news source.

Principles of Successful Media Relations

- All media are not the same. Know the differences and use each to your advantage.
- Honor deadlines. Give the media enough prior notice so that they can schedule someone to cover your event.
- Avoid technical and bureaucratic jargon. The media are your bridge to the public. They cannot convey your message if they do not understand it.
- Be honest. Never be afraid to say, "I don't know," but add "I'll find out for you."
- Make people in your agency or organization available as experts for background information or interviews.
- Remember that one picture is worth a thousand words, but you may have to stage that photo opportunity yourself, or have your staff prepare clear graphics.
- Write clearly and succinctly, following the who-what-when-where-how formula.
- Submit all written material neatly typed, double-spaced, with all names, dates, and places double-checked for accuracy.
- Prepare media kits to distribute to reporters who come to your meeting, and to those who stay away.
- Look for less obvious publicity niches to reach segments of the public that are important to your agency or the event.
- Know your local editors, station or program managers, and reporters and encourage them to assign one person to cover your agency or organization consistently.
- Dress appropriately when the camera is or might be any-where in sight.
- Face the inevitable — bad news does indeed drive out good news — but take that as a challenge to convince the media otherwise.
- Be friendly with the media, but do not expect the media to be your friends. Everyone has a job to do, and the public is best served if each one does it well.

9

Step-by-Step Checklist for Meeting Planners

If there is one lesson that executives and their staffs should always remember about organizing public meetings, it is never to leave anything to chance—or the last minute. This checklist, divided into premeeting, meeting, and postmeeting phases, should help you cover everything. It assumes that you are planning a public meeting for fifty to one hundred people. The same steps are needed for a smaller or larger group, though the exact details and amount of staff and other resources will differ, of course.

Premeeting

- Set aside sufficient time and resources for planning the meeting. Two months or six weeks ahead is not too soon, especially if the appropriate space is popular and should be reserved well in advance or if there are several presenters and audiovisuals that need to be coordinated.
- Indicate the importance that top management assigns to the event by attending key planning meetings: one or more at

the beginning, when the goals and objectives, format, and presenters are chosen, and the final rehearsals.

- Appoint a staff committee with a chair or manager responsible for overseeing the entire event. Include on that committee all presenters except experts or consultants brought in from the outside, graphics or audiovisual preparers, at least one secretary or clerical assistant to take minutes and keep lists of tasks and responsibilities, and anyone else — perhaps a friendly citizen or political ally — who may have special knowledge of the subject, of the audience, or of controversial issues that should be covered. The core group should work together throughout the entire planning and execution phases.

- At your first get-together, agree on the purpose of the meeting — informational, advisory, or problem solving — and design the format to accommodate your goals. Never promise more to the public than you are willing or able to deliver. For example, do not set up a problem-solving meeting when you have no intention of changing your plan or project in response to suggestions that citizens might have. It is more credible and acceptable to tell the audience that the meeting is purely informational.

- In your planning, always keep in mind the likely expectations of the audience, even in deciding how long the meeting should be. Except for half- or full-day workshops, most public meetings become unproductive after two or two and one-half hours. It is better to end on a high note, or even agree to have another meeting, than to wear out everyone.

- Decide early in the planning where you will hold the meeting and make the appropriate arrangements. Assign someone to visit the site to make certain that it meets your requirements.

- List everything that needs to get done and agree on responsibilities and deadlines. Distribute the schedule to everyone involved.

- Make a floor plan of the meeting room and decide where each graphic will go. This eases the necessity of having to make major decisions at the last minute, though a certain flexibility is necessary to meet unexpected situations.

- Meet regularly — at least once a week — to review roles and responsibilities, report on progress, and make adjustments to the schedule when necessary. The agency executive does not need to attend all these meetings but should be apprised of any major problems that arise.
- Begin to develop concepts for graphics as soon as the subject of the various presentations is decided. Write and review an outline of any slide show or video; then write and review the script. Finally, prepare a "story board" or photo/script outline. If several levels of content review are required, build them into your schedule.
- Review drafts of all oral presentations, maps, and charts to make sure that they are consistent, clear, and concise. Hold this review sufficiently ahead of time that appropriate changes can be made.
- Develop or refine your mailing list. Who must be notified legally? Who should be notified to show your agency's goodwill and openness? Design your mailings carefully according to criteria discussed in Chapter Three. If you have no legal requirements for timing, mailing ten days or two weeks ahead is adequate. Do not notify people too much in advance or they will forget. If you can afford two mailings, send the first three weeks ahead and send the follow-up a week ahead.
- Make a list of those who should receive special notes or reminder calls and assign someone to take care of that. VIPs may require a personal telephone call or a letter from the agency director or a high-prestige political officeholder. Your VIP list may include leaders of key organizations, political influentials, and important personnel within your or other agencies.
- Assign someone to be in charge of media relations for this event. Even if your agency has a public information person, the meeting may be important enough to have an individual specially assigned to the task. It is to your advantage to begin early to develop ideas for special coverage and to cultivate those media representatives who may be particularly receptive.

- Order the refreshments, taking into account your budget and the expectations and preferences of your audience.
- Make logistical assignments — drivers and vans to transport bulky equipment, site manager and troubleshooter, registrars, someone to post signs, and a general gofer.
- Prepare a complete inventory of all materials and equipment and test to make sure that everything is in working order.
- Stock a meeting kit that contains at least the following: paper, pens, pencils, marking pens, chalk, name tags, extra projector bulbs, extension cords, tape, and aspirin.
- About a week before the meeting, hold a dry run in your office conference room to review everything that will be said and done. Include the people who participated in your early planning sessions but who have not been involved in subsequent day-to-day activities. Make notes of any changes that you agree upon and make sure that they are made.
- To assure uniformity and quality control, write a guide for discussion leaders that includes the issues that they should cover. Hold a training session to review what is expected.
- A day ahead (or a few hours, if you cannot use the room much beforehand), hold a dress rehearsal on the site. This will do much to allay your fears and stage fright and will reveal the inevitable problems — charts that need bigger titles in order to be read, awkward positioning for the projector and screen, electrical outlets that do not work — enough in advance that you can do something about them.
- Arrive early to set up everything according to plan.

During the Meeting

- Start at the appointed time. If all your planning has been sufficient and you have taken care of everything noted in this book, you should be on your way to a successful session that satisfies you and your audience. The site manager should be poised to take care of the inevitable last-minute problems.
- End on time. Honor the pact that you made with all the participants but offer to stay later to accommodate anyone who has additional questions.

Postmeeting

- At the beginning of the planning, when you make up your meeting schedule, include a time for recap and evaluation not more than a day or two afterward. Invite everyone who participated in the planning and execution. You may also want to include interested outsiders, for more dispassionate opinions.
- The meeting should be chaired by the agency executive and include a candid discussion of everything that occurred. The original outline of purpose and goals should provide the bench mark. Did the meeting reach or exceed your expectations? What did you learn that will help you carry out the project or program? What was the reaction of the public? Are other meetings necessary? Should you schedule additional follow-up, such as letters or telephone calls, to specific groups or individuals? Was the media coverage adequate or what you expected? If there were any problems with the media, how should they be handled? What worked particularly well? What should be improved upon next time?
- Choose individuals to carry out postmeeting activities.
- Assign someone to write a summary evaluation of the meeting as a guide for the future.
- Give praise where warranted. There should be enough to go around.

Suggestions for Further Reading

Bernstein, T. M. *The Careful Writer*. New York: Atheneum, 1965.

Carpenter, S. L., and Kennedy, W.J.D. *Managing Public Disputes: A Practical Guide to Handling Conflict and Reaching Agreements*. San Francisco: Jossey-Bass, 1988.

Cogan, A., Sharpe, S., and Hertzberg, J. *The Practice of State and Regional Planning (Citizen Participation)*. Chicago: American Planning Association with the International City Management Association, 1986.

Cogan, E., and Padrow, B. *You Can Talk to (Almost) Anyone About (Almost) Anything*. Portland, Oreg.: Continuing Education Publications, Portland State University, 1984.

Cogan & Associates. *Techniques of Public Involvement*. Washington, D.C.: Council of State Planning Agencies, 1977.

Doyle, M., and Straus, D. *How to Make Meetings Work*. New York: Berkley, 1984.

Fletcher, W. *Meetings, Meetings*. New York: Morrow, 1984.

O'Hayre, J. *Gobbledygook Has Gotta Go*. Washington, D.C.: U.S. Government Printing Office, 1966.

Robert, H. N. *Robert's Rules of Order*. New York: Bell, 1907.

Stacey, W. S. *Business and Professional Speaking*. New York: William C. Brown, 1983.

Strauss, B., and Strauss, F. *New Ways to Better Meetings*. New York: Viking, 1952.

Index

133